Young Women Fun-tastic! Personal Progress Motivators

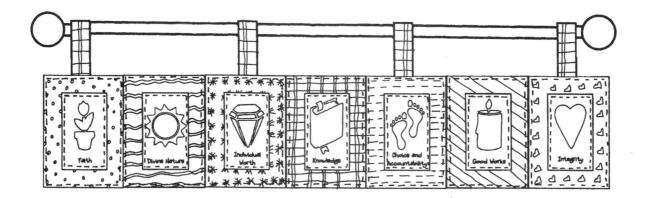

Each of the Seven Value Themes Contain:

❀ Midweek Motivational Activities

❀ Fun Ways to Teach Values

❀ Invitations and Certificates

❀ 8 Mirror Motivators
(Value Experience Planners and Project Planner
To Plan the Personal Progress Goals and Project)

❀ Stenciled Value Quilt

Covenant Communications, Inc.
American Fork, Utah

Printed in the United States of America
First Printing: July, 2002

Young Women Fun-tastic! Personal Progress Motivators
ISBN: 1-59156-051-9

ACKNOWLEDGEMENTS: Thanks to Inspire Graphics www.inspiregraphichs.com
for the use of Lettering Delights computer fonts

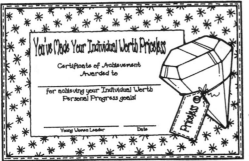

INTRODUCTION

Personal Progress Motivators

The Personal Progress Program is an inspired Program for young women to achieve goals in the seven value areas. Young Women leaders or parents, you can use these Personal Progress Motivators to inspire young women to achieve their goals and enrich their lives.

This Book Contains:

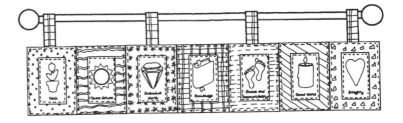

❀ *7 Midweek Motivation Activities* representing the young women values: Faith, Divine Nature, Individual Worth, Knowledge, Choice and Accountability, Good Works, and Integrity.

❀ 7 invitations for the *Motivation Activities* (sample below).

❀ Fun Ways to Teach Values during these *Midweek Motivational Activities*. You will also find additional handouts and activities (previewed) that can be printed from the *Personal Progress* CD-ROM*. These will add to and enhance the presentations you make. See *Preview of Motivational Handouts* on the next page.

❀ 7 award certificates for achieving Personal Progress goals in the seven values (sample above).

❀ 8 Mirror Motivators (Value Experience planners and Value Project planners) for each of the seven values.

❀ 7 quilt patterns to stencil a Value Quilt (shown above) to reward young women for completing their goals in the seven value areas (see Appendix).

Each Value Motivational Activity Includes the Following:

Invitation:

Send a week ahead (sample right).

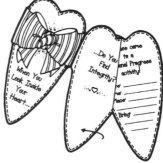

Goal Planners—Mirror Motivators:

When the young women arrive, introduce the goals for that value and give each young woman a planner form for goals #1-7 and the value project (shown left and right). Encourage young women to post these planners on their mirror to motivate them. The planners are like worksheets that map out their goals step by step. Talk about each goal and ask young women to share the experiences they have had while achieving these goals. Help each young woman choose a value project and plan it on the *Value Project Planner* (sample shown right).

• Fun Ways to Teach Values:

To add to and enhance your Midweek Motivational Activity, choose from these activities to motivate goal achievement. All of these relate to specific goals in that value area, e.g., for the Faith Goal #1 we suggest you can have a *Scripture Seek and Run* or a *Scripture Bowl* to get them excited about the scriptures. For Goal #3 you can motivate them to practice the gospel principle of fasting with the *Fasting Facts* activity, or practice the gospel principle of repentance with the *Mighty Change of Heart* activity.

Preview of Motivational Handouts:

Along with the hundreds of Midweek Motivational Activities, you will find previews of motivational handouts. These are available to print from the *Personal Progress Motivators* CD-ROM*. They are also found in the *Young Women Fun-tastic! Activities* books and CD-ROM for manuals 1, 2, and 3. These motivational handouts help teach gospel subjects and motivate goal achievement. For example, the *Eternal Marriage Puzzle Quiz* (shown right) motivates young women to marry in the temple. This matches with the *Choice and Accountability Value Experience Planner #6 "Preparing to Enter the Temple,"* (shown left).

Plan Ahead:
With so many *Fun Ways to Teach Values*, you could plan six years ahead, choosing specific activities each year for each Midweek Motivational Activity, so the activities wouldn't be repeated. Forms could be copied once for each young woman, then new forms copied as young women come into the program.

Group Workshops:
During the Midweek Motivational Activity you could have young women in four different rooms rotating, covering two Value Experiences in each, and awarding certificates.

Quick-Print Option:
This book is available on CD-ROM* to print all of the images shown in this book in full color or black and white (shown left). See samples on the back of this book.

*All images shown in this book can be printed in color or black and white from the *Young Women Fun-tastic! Personal Progress Motivators* CD-ROM.

Young Women Value-able Journal:

Create a *Young Women Value-able Journal* for each young woman to store Value Experience planners, Value Project planners, and motivational handouts. Place the cover (shown below) and divider pages with tabs (shown right) in a binder to help them organize. They can then pull out the planners and handouts to post on the mirror and to work on them, replacing them in the journal when the work is complete.

In the Appendix you will find the cover (shown below) and the tabs (shown right). You can also copy or print the seven young women value divider pages (shown right) from the *Personal Progress Motivators* CD-ROM* or the *Young Women Fun-tastic! Activities, Manuals 1, 2, and 3* books and CD-ROMs.

If you don't print the value divider pages from the CD-ROM,* you can attach the value tabs on value-colored cardstock paper to match the value colors and floral symbols found on the tabs and divider pages. The value colors are: Faith (white), Divine Nature (blue), Individual Worth (red), Knowledge (yellow), Choice and Accountability (orange), Good Works (green), and Integrity (purple).

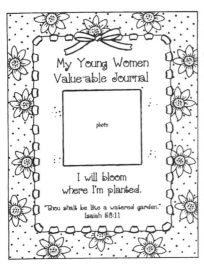

You can help young women identify the floral symbols found on the handouts previewed in this book (found on the CD-ROM*). The floral symbols show young women where to place their handouts in the journal; placing them behind the matching floral tab (see above and below). Example, the orange poppy on the handout (shown below/left) shows young women where to place this handout in their journal.

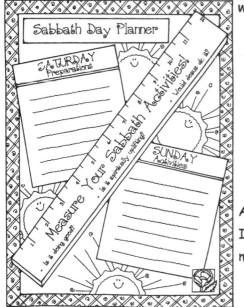

The Floral Symbols Are: Faith (white lily), Choice & Accountability (orange poppy), Good Works (yellow sunflower), Integrity (purple pansy), Knowledge (green ivy), Divine Nature (blue morning glory), and Individual Worth (red rose).

TABLE OF CONTENTS
Young Women Fun-tastic! Personal Progress Motivators

Each of These Midweek Motivational Activities Contain:

❀ Invitations and Award Certificates

❀ 8 Mirror Motivators

(Value Experience Planners and Project Planner

To Plan the Personal Progress Goals and Project)

❀ Fun Ways to Teach Values

❀ Value Quilt and Journal

Midweek Motivational Activities:

Value: Faith
Theme: Our Faith Grows as We Follow Jesus Christ

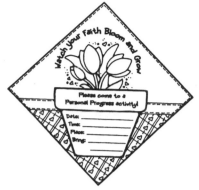

Invitation and Certificates: (1) *Copy the invitation and certificate (page 6) for each young woman. (2) *Color and cut out images and fill in details. (3) To make invitation, cut slits on sides and insert, and glue or tape tabs on the back to make a 3-D flower pot. Deliver a week ahead. (4) See #5 below to distribute certificate.

Goal Planning and Sharing: You'll need a *copy of the Faith Value Experience #1-7 planners and the Faith Value Project Planner (pages 7-14) for each young woman.

DISTRIBUTE FORMS AND HAVE ONE OR MORE ACTIVITIES FROM THE FOLLOWING PAGES, "FUN WAYS TO TEACH VALUES":

1. Tell young women that, We are daughters of Heavenly Father, who loves us. We have faith in His eternal plan, which centers on Jesus Christ, our Savior. Read Alma 32:21 (shown on page 12 in the Personal Progress booklet).

2. Give each young woman a set of Faith Value Experience #1-7 planners and a Value Project Planner (sample shown left). Review each planner #1-7 titles, e.g., #1: "*My Faith Grows as I Learn from the Scriptures and the Living Prophets.*"

3. Suggest that they use the planners as worksheets to plan and carry out their goals and as a journal to record their experiences. When young women have passed off their goals, they can record these in their Personal Progress journal, if desired.

4. Suggest that they post the planners on the mirror as a reminder. When complete, store them in a looseleaf notebook or folder (see Introduction).

5. Award a Faith certificate and a quilt block to young women who have achieved all their Faith goals. See the Appendix to make the quilt.

*All images shown in this book can be printed in color or black and white from the *Young Women Fun-tastic! Personal Progress Motivators* CD-ROM.

Fun Ways to Teach Values:

Choose one or more of the following activities to motivate goal achievement.

FAITH — VALUE EXPERIENCE #1: SCRIPTURES

SEARCH AND PONDER BOOKMARK:

To Make: Print the pattern (shown left) from the *Personal Progress CD-ROM**. Copy or print the pattern from the *Young Women Fun-tastic! Activities – Manual 1* book or CD-ROM (Lesson #27). *Color and cut out.

Activity: Give each young woman a *Search and Ponder* bookmark and review the steps to make scripture reading more meaningful. Ask them to try following these steps each day for one week and share their experiences the following week.

SCRIPTURE CHALLENGE BOOKMARK WITH TESTIMONY JOURNAL:

To Make: Print the patterns (shown right) from the *Personal Progress CD-ROM**. Or, copy or print the patterns from the *Young Women Fun-tastic! Activities – Manual 3* book or CD-ROM (Lesson #30). *Color, cut out, and glue back to-back.

Activity: Give each young woman a bookmark and testimony journal to challenge them to read the scriptures daily. Ask them to read the scripture assigned on the bookmark each day, e.g., on Monday, read 2 Nephi 4:15. Then draw a heart shape in the box next to each scripture read. Encourage them to write key words from the scripture to summarize that scripture in the space below.

Challenge Personal Study: Challenge young women to start or continue a personal scripture study program, and pray for the Spirit of the Holy Ghost to guide them as they read. *Encourage Testimony:* Ask them to write their testimony of scripture study on side two of the bookmark.

SCRIPTURE SEEK AND RUN:

Create a challenging scripture game where young women search the scriptures in teams and run to find clues taped to the walls before time is up.

To Make Game: Before activity, have young women class presidents and leaders get together. Search the scriptures together and write questions on slips of paper. On a separate paper, write clues that provide the answers (to be taped to walls around the activity room.) Sample Question: In 1 Nephi 13:9, what destroys the saints of God and brings them down into captivity? Clue card: "the _ _ _ _ _ _ of the world." The answer and missing word is "praise."

To Play: You'll need a watch with a second hand. Divide young women into teams and take turns drawing a question. Each team has 1 minute to find the scripture and the clue taped to the wall. If they can't do this, the other team has 1 minute to find the answer. If the second team can't

*All images shown in this book can be printed in color or black and white from the
Young Women Fun-tastic! Personal Progress Motivators CD-ROM.

find it, the first team tries again. The team with the most clue cards completed wins.
Rules: The one-minute time starts after the question is read. The team that is not participating does not open their scriptures until it is their turn. Scriptures must be closed at the beginning of each question. Write in a few missing words as a clue after one minute is up.

SCRIPTURE BOWL:

Have a bowl filled with scriptures and scripture questions. Young women can divide into teams and race to find the answer, taking turns choosing a question from the bowl. If it is easy to find you don't need to include a scripture (see Example #1) that follows. If it is difficult to find, include the scripture (see Example #2) that follows. The first team to find and read the answer wins!

Example #1: "Who was King Benjamin's father?" Don't include the reference. They can find this by looking for "Benjamin" in the Index to find Omni 1:23 to learn that Mosiah is the answer.

Example #2: "How can I know if the Book of Mormon is true?" (see Moroni 10:4-5).

❀ *Option #1:* Have dads or bishopric team up with or compete with young women to find the answers.

❀ *Option #2:* Young women can come with ten of their favorite scriptures to share in the scripture chase.

FAITH — VALUE EXPERIENCE #2 and #3: DISCOVER AND LIVE GOSPEL PRINCIPLES

Value Experience #3 suggests that young women prepare a family home evening on how faith helps them live gospel principles. See the *Family Home Evening Resource* book, published by The Church. The following activities could also be presented along with a lesson.

❀ *Gospel Principle: Repentance*
See Choice and Accountability — Value Experience #4
❀ *Gospel Principle: Eternal Life*
See Knowledge — Value Experience #4
❀ *Gospel Principle: Honesty*
See Divine Nature — Value Experience #6
❀ *Gospel Principle: Fasting*
See Integrity — Value Experience #6

❀ *Gospel Principle: Sabbath Day*

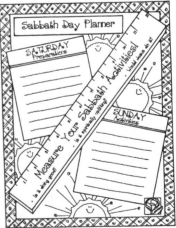

SABBATH DAY PLANNER:

To Make: Print the pattern (shown right) from the *Personal Progress CD-ROM**. Or, copy or print the pattern from the *Young Women Fun-tastic! Activities - Manual 1* book or CD-ROM (Lesson #25). *Color.

Activity: Give each young woman a *Sabbath Day Planner* to think about how they measuring up to Sabbath day activities. Talk About: Are the activities doing good? Are they spiritually uplifting? Would Jesus do

*All images shown in this book can be printed in color or black and white from the
Young Women Fun-tastic! Personal Progress Motivators CD-ROM.

3

these activities on the Sabbath? Young women can write what they can do on Saturday to prepare for the Sabbath and the activities they will do on Sunday that keep the Sabbath day holy. You could make multiple copies of the *Sabbath Day Planner* so young women can present it in a family home evening lesson.

SABBATH DAY SHOW-AND-TELL IDEA NIGHT:

Have young women bring games and activities they like to do with their family. They can present a family home evening idea, gospel game (or any game their family enjoys), scripture activities, and more.

Sabbath Day Ideas: Bible Bingo (make up your own game), scripture chase, sharing time lessons from the *Friend,* thumbprint pictures of animals found in the scriptures; share journal entries, review missionary discussions, write letters to missionaries or family and friends, tell stories about ancestors or about an ancestor's possession with show-and-tell, make a gospel grab bag by looking up favorite scriptures and placing them in a bag (young women can draw them out of a bag and try to guess the young woman who wrote the scripture). Young women can also make a testimony time capsule by writing testimonies, burying them in a container, and digging them up before graduating from the Young Women program. With these ideas and those of your young women, you should be able to make each Sabbath day memorable.

❀ *Gospel Principle: Forgiveness*

FORGIVENESS BITE-SIZE MEMORIZE POSTER:

Give young women this Ephesians 4:32 bite-size memorize poster to memorize and learn the importance of forgiving others. Role-play forgiving situations. Divide young women into two groups to role-play situations where forgiveness is needed and how the other person forgives. Talk about how a situation might turn out if someone did not forgive. How would they feel in days, weeks, months, and years to come?

To Make: Print the pattern (shown left) from the *Personal Progress CD-ROM**. Or, copy or print the pattern from the *Young Women Fun-tastic! Activities – Manual 1* book or CD-ROM (Lesson #23). *Color.

FORGIVE AND FORGET-ME-"KNOT":

1. Give each young woman an 8-inch piece of string and ask someone to tie it on her finger with a knot. Say, "When we don't forgive others, our spirit gets tied up in 'knots' and our spirit isn't free to love that person."

2. Ask young women to untie the knot on their neighbor's finger. Say, "When we forgive, we need to forget and let go. When we can forgive and forget, we find inner peace, and the person we forgive will also."

3. Tie the knot again on their fingers and have them wear the string home as a reminder "knot" to forget to forgive others.

*All images shown in this book can be printed in color or black and white from the
Young Women Fun-tastic! Personal Progress Motivators CD-ROM.

4

FORGIVING HEARTS, LETTING GO!:

Have young women write on a heart shaped note something they are truly willing to let go of (a hurt, bad feelings about someone, etc.). Discuss how when we don't forgive, our heart and mind cannot move on to more important things. Forgiveness frees our spirit, leaving room for love and friendship. Have each young woman tie her note to a helium balloon and let it go, letting go of the hurt and bad feeling. Serve heart shaped cookies with "forgiving heart" written on each.

RED ROSE PEACE OFFERING:

Say, "The yellow hybrid tea rose is known as a symbol of peace. It was smuggled in from France in 1942 and given out at the United Nations meeting in 1945 that marked the end of the war."

To Make: Print the pattern (shown right) from the *Personal Progress CD-ROM** for each young woman to give to a friend or family member in order to make peace. *Color the rose yellow.

> This rose represents my friendship and love. It symbolizes peace. I'm sorry if I have ever offended you or mistreated you. I love you!
>
> Love,

FAITH — VALUE EXPERIENCE #4 and #5: SACRAMENT

See Divine Nature — Value Experience #4: Take upon the Name of Jesus Christ: Last Supper

FAITH — VALUE EXPERIENCE #6: PLAN OF SALVATION

PLAN OF SALVATION FAMILY HOME EVENING:

The Faith Personal Progress Goal #6 suggests that young women draw or obtain a picture that depicts the plan of salvation (as follows) and explain the plan of salvation.

To Make: Print the *Plan of Salvation Story Board* figures and wordstrips (shown right) from the *Personal Progress CD-ROM** for each young woman.

To Present: Young women can place images on the wall or a poster board with tape as they read the scriptures found in the Faith Goal #6 as follows: 2 Nephi 9:1-28, 11:4-7, Moses 4:1-4, Revelation 12:7-9, D&C 76:50-113, 93:33-34, Abraham 3:24-27, and 1 Corinthians 15:22.

*All images shown in this book can be printed in color or black and white from the
Young Women Fun-tastic! Personal Progress Motivators CD-ROM.

Watch your Faith Bloom and Grow

Please come to a
Personal Progress activity!

Date:
Time:
Place:
Bring:

your Faith Is Blooming All over the Place

Certificate of Achievement
Awarded to

_____

for achieving your
Faith Personal Progress goals!

_____
young Women Leader   Date

My Faith Grows as I Learn from the Scriptures and the Living Prophets

Faith — Value Experience #1:

SEARCH AND PONDER: How These Scriptures Relate to Me:

Hebrews 11 _____

_____

Alma 32:17-42 _____

_____

Ether 12:6-22 _____

_____

Joseph Smith—History 1:11-20 _____

_____

After Reading and Pondering Two General Conference Talks on Faith, this Is How They Relate to Me:

Talk #1: _____ by: _____

_____

_____

_____

Talk #2: _____ by: _____

_____

_____

_____

I Exercised Faith by Praying Morning and Evening for Three Weeks:

Week #1 M__ __   T__ __   W__ __   T__ __   F__ __   S__ __   S__ __

Week #2 M__ __   T__ __   W__ __   T__ __   F__ __   S__ __   S__ __

Week #3 M__ __   T__ __   W__ __   T__ __   F__ __   S__ __   S__ __

Discover Principles of Faith Taught by the Mothers of Helaman's Stripling Warriors

Faith – Value Experience #2:

SEARCH AND PONDER:

Alma 56:45-48 and 57:21

These Are the Principles of Faith These Mothers Taught Their Sons:

_____

_____

_____

Review "The Family: A Proclamation to the World"
(see Personal Progress Book, page ii).
What it Says about a Mother's Role:

_____

_____

_____

_____

I Discussed with Someone the Following Qualities a Woman Needs to Teach
Children to Have Faith and to Base Their Decisions on Gospel Truths:

_____

How These Principles Help Me Prepare to Be
A Mother and Help Me in My Life Today.

_____

_____

_____

_____

Teach Others How Faith Helps
Us Live Gospel Principles

Faith – Value Experience #3:

I Planned and Presented a Family Home Evening

on the Following Gospel Subject*:

_____

I taught how faith helps us live this gospel principle as follows:

_____

_____

_____

_____

_____

Experiences Shared by Me or My Family:

_____

_____

_____

_____

_____

*Gospel Principles: prayer, tithing, fasting, repentance,
keeping the Sabbath day holy

Learn More About the Sacrament

Faith – Value Experience #4:

SEARCH AND PONDER

the Last Supper:

Matthew 26:26-28, Mark 14:22-24, and Luke 22:17-20.

For Three Weeks I Listened to the Sacrament Hymns and Prayers,
Thinking about Why I Partake of the Bread and Water.

Week #1 _____ Week #2 _____ Week #3 _____

Promises I Make as I Partake of the Sacrament
And Remember My Baptismal Covenants:

_____

_____

_____

_____

_____

_____

Promise Ideas: Obey the Commandments, Read the Scriptures,
Honor Parents, Serve Others, Pay Tithing, Attend Church Meetings.
Heavenly Father Promises to: Forgive Me When I Repent,
Love and Bless Me, Give Me the Gift of the Holy Ghost, Answer My Prayers,
Let Me Live with Him Forever.

Increase Understanding of the Atonement

Faith – Value Experience #5:

SEARCH AND PONDER:

My Feelings about the Savior and What
He Has Done for Me After Reading:

Isaiah 53:3-12 _____

_____

_____

John 3:16-17 _____

_____

_____

Romans 5 _____

_____

_____

2 Nephi 9:6-7; 21-26 _____

_____

_____

_____

Alma 7:11-13; 34:8-17 _____

_____

_____

_____

Doctrine and Covenants 19:15-20 _____

_____

_____

Learn about the Plan of Salvation

Faith – Value Experience #6:

SEARCH AND PONDER:

I Obtained or Drew a Picture of the Plan of Salvation*.
Using These Pictures I Explained the Plan of Salvation
to My Class, Family, or Friend as Follows:

2 Nephi 9:1-28 _____

_____

2 Nephi 11:4-7 _____

_____

Moses 4:1-4 _____

_____

Revelation 12:7-9 _____

_____

Doctrine and Covenants 76:50-113 _____

_____

Doctrine and Covenants 93:33-34 _____

_____

Abraham 3:24-27 _____

_____

1 Corinthians 15:22 _____

_____

*Plan of Salvation Includes: premortal existence, birth, mortal life,
death, judgement, and life after judgement

Learn about the
Commandment of Tithing

Faith – Value Experience #7:

SEARCH AND PONDER

Summary of Scriptures–How the Lord Has Commanded Us to Pay:

Doctrine and Covenants 119 and Malachi 3:8-12

_____

_____

_____

To Show My Obedience I Paid My Tithing for Three Months:

Month #1: _____   Month #2: _____   Month #3: _____

How Paying My Tithing Has Helped My Faith Grow:

_____

_____

_____

_____

_____

Faith Value Project Planner

My Project Is:

_____

_____

_____

_____

Steps to Carry Out My Project:

1. _____
2. _____
3. _____
4. _____
5. _____
6. _____
7. _____
8. _____

How I Felt about the Project:

_____

_____

How My Understanding of Faith Increased with this Project:

_____

_____

Midweek Motivational Activities:

Value: Divine Nature
Theme: We Have Divine Qualities We Can Develop

Invitation and Certificates: (1) *Copy the invitation and certificate (pages 27-28) for each young woman. (2) *Color and cut out images and fill in details. (3) To make invitation, cut out the cloud in the center and insert sun. Deliver a week ahead. (4) See #5 below to distribute certificate.

Goal Planning and Sharing: You'll need a *copy of the Divine Nature Value Experience #1-7 planners and the Divine Nature Value Project Planner (pages 29-36) for each young woman.

DISTRIBUTE FORMS AND HAVE ONE OR MORE ACTIVITIES FROM THE FOLLOWING PAGES "FUN WAYS TO TEACH VALUES":

1. Tell young women that we have inherited divine qualities as we are daughters of God. Read 2 Peter 1:4-7 (shown on page 19 in the Personal Progress booklet).

2. Give each young woman a set of Divine Nature Value Experience #1-7 planners and a Value Project Planner (sample shown left). Review each planner #1-7 titles, e.g., #1: *"Discover and Build Upon Your Divine Qualities as You Are a Daughter of God."*

3. Suggest that they use the planners as worksheets to plan and carry out their goals and as a journal to record their experiences. When the young women have passed off their goals, they can record these in their Personal Progress journal, if desired.

4. Suggest that they post the planners on the mirror as a reminder. When complete, store them in a looseleaf notebook or folder (see Introduction).

5. Award a Divine Nature certificate and a quilt block to young women who have achieved all their Divine Nature goals. See the Appendix to make the quilt.

*All images shown in this book can be printed in color or black and white from the
Young Women Fun-tastic! Personal Progress Motivators CD-ROM.

Fun Ways to Teach Values:

Choose one or more of the following activities to motivate goal achievement.

DIVINE NATURE — VALUE EXPERIENCE #1: DAUGHTER OF GOD DIVINE QUALITIES

DRAWING NEARER TO MY HEAVENLY FATHER GOAL POSTER:

To Make: Print the pattern (shown left) from the *Personal Progress* CD-ROM*. Or, copy or print the pattern from the *Young Women Fun-tastic! Activities – Manual 1* book or CD-ROM (Lesson #1). *Color.

Activity: Using the *Drawing Nearer to My Heavenly Father* goal poster, help young women think of ways they can improve their relationship with their Heavenly Father. Study the following scriptures to learn that we show our love to Heavenly Father by keeping his commandments and by serving others. Have young women write on the poster how they will draw closer to Heavenly Father. See Lesson #1 in the *Young Women* lesson manual 1 for ideas. *Scriptures:* D&C 88:63, Mosiah 2:17, John 14:15, and Matthew 25:40.

MEDITATION MOMENTS:

Find a special place, (a park, a mountain stream, or beautiful meadow) away from crowds (dress warm in the winter). Have young women listen for several minutes without speaking, then discuss the silence. Ask, "When was the last time you did something like this?" Talk about distractions (e.g., TV, radio, cars, people, children, etc.). Express the importance of meditation and prayer. Ask if Joseph Smith could have received his first vision in his home, a house full of people coming and going, instead of in the Sacred Grove. Express the importance of meditating, and listening to the Spirit for inspiration and answers.

RED CARPET ROLL-UPS TREAT:

Give young women a red fruit roll-up. Tell them they are of royal birth and part of Heavenly Father's kingdom so you are "rolling out the red carpet for them," which is how people treat royalty. Each day give yourself the red carpet treatment and treat yourself royally by obeying the commandments.

HEAVENLY PHONE CALL CROSSMATCH:

To Make: Print the pattern (left) from the *Personal Progress* CD-ROM*. Or, copy or print the pattern from the *Young Women Fun-tastic! – Manual 1* book or CD-ROM (Lesson #24). *Color.

Activity: Tell young women that "a prayer, like a simple phone call, can be made each day to Heavenly Father." Have young women do the *Heavenly Phone Call* crossmatch activity to learn how prayer will help. *Answers:* Say "Prayers will help us build a testimony, overcome negative attitudes, observe a meaningful fast, withstand peer group pressures, maintain Church standards, solve school problems, improve one's self-image, keep the Word of Wisdom, develop good habits, and overcome weaknesses."

*All images shown in this book can be printed in color or black and white from the
Young Women Fun-tastic! Personal Progress Motivators CD-ROM.

16

DIVINE NATURE — VALUE EXPERIENCE #2: QUALITY WIFE AND MOTHER

FAMILY LIFE CAN BE A PICNIC TENT CARD:

To Make: Print the pattern (shown right) from the *Personal Progress* CD-ROM*. Or, copy or print the pattern from the *Young Women Fun-tastic! Activities – Manual 1* book or CD-ROM (Lesson #8). *Color and cut out and fold to stand up.

Activity: Help young women realize that attitude is the key to a happy home. Life can be a "picnic" (or at least, a lot easier) if we have the right attitude. Encourage young women to write on this tent card those roles of a wife and mother that help make family life more enjoyable. They can practice creating a positive environment while they are living at home. Then when they are living with roommates or have a home of their own, they will be in the habit of creating a positive environment, where friendship and love can endure.

"MY MAN" WISH LIST:

Have young women brainstorm about what kind of man they would like to marry. Make this a long list. Then check all qualities that really matter, crossing out or erasing the not-so-necessary qualifications. Last, ask the girls if they think they themselves possess these traits. Explain that we can't expect something of someone if we are not willing to be that too (see D&C 88:40).

A MAN'S OPINION PANEL:

Have a panel of husbands and young men. Ask them to share their thoughts about their wives or mothers and what makes the "best" mom or a "great" wife. Prepare questions ahead of time to ask panel.

POSITIVE TRAITS TO ATTRACT A POSITIVE MATE! DECISION TENT CARD:

To Make: Print the pattern (shown right) from the *Personal Progress* CD-ROM*. Or, copy or print the pattern from the *Young Women Fun-tastic! Activities – Manual 3* book or CD-ROM (Lesson #36). *Color, cut out and fold.

Activity: (1) From one side of the tent-card, help young women memorize the quote: "Marriage is perhaps the most vital of all decisions," by Spencer W. Kimball, and talk about making that important decision now and when the opportunity for marriage comes. (2) On the other side of the tent-card, have young women list the positive traits they would like in their future husband. Also have them list what they want to be. This list could match, showing the same qualities to develop. Remind young women that if they want to date and marry a person with the qualities they desire, they too must acquire these qualities. This way they will attract that type of individual to them (D&C 88:40).

*All images shown in this book can be printed in color or black and white from the
Young Women Fun-tastic! Personal Progress Motivators CD-ROM.

INTERNATIONAL NIGHT:

Have several women of different nationalities come and talk about their roles as wives and mothers. Have visitors express their feelings about their callings as wives and mothers, and the influence the world has. Discuss the similarities in their roles as they strive to do what their Heavenly Father wants them to do. Have refreshments from the different nationalities (include recipes).

FAMILY UNITY CHECKLIST:

To Make: Print the pattern (shown left) from the *Personal Progress CD-ROM**. Or, copy or print the pattern from the *Young Women Fun-tastic! Activities – Manual 3* book or CD-ROM (Lesson #9). *Color.

Activity: Ask young women to use this *Family Unity Checklist* to list things they can do this coming week to create family unity (family ties). Read Mosiah 18:8-9 with the young women and discuss the advantages of serving in their family. *Color.

TEACH HOW TO BUILD FAMILY SELF-ESTEEM:

Tell young women that we are self-image builders. Before the workshop, have someone who is a builder prepare some precut boards; have nails, hammers, scotch tape, string, and glue available. Have young women in groups build a project without nails. Give them scotch tape, string, and glue. Demonstrate how the finished project is shaky and may not stand up under pressure. Bring out nails and hammer, and proceed to redo it using nails. The project is now much more sturdy. Discuss our ability to supply "nails" (strong support) in building up others or our building our self-image. If we supply only a tape, glue, or string type of support, the support doesn't last. Discuss situations that build confidence. Create a favor by nailing two boards together and then nailing this note to the board: "When times get tough and you need to be strong, you can draw on your inner strength. Build yourself and your family to withstand life's challenges."

DIVINE NATURE — VALUE EXPERIENCE #3:
MAKE HOME LIFE BETTER
Also see Knowledge — Value Experience #5

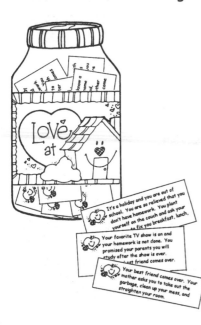

LOVE AT HOME SPIN-THE-BOTTLE:

To Make: Print the pattern (shown left) from the *Personal Progress CD-ROM**. Or, copy or print the pattern from the *Young Women Fun-tastic! Activities – Manual 2* book or CD-ROM (Lesson #7). *Color and cut out label and wordstrips. Glue label on a bottle and enclose wordstrips.

Activity: Young women spin the bottle. When the bottleneck points to them, they read a wordstrip and tell how they would show love in the situation found on the wordstrip.

*All images shown in this book can be printed in color or black and white from the
Young Women Fun-tastic! Personal Progress Motivators CD-ROM.

18

FAMILY DELEGATION:

Plan a picnic with the young women and play volleyball. Let them make plans and delegate assignments. Have some "forget" their assignment, e.g., forget the napkins; forget utensils and bring only the knife, so young women must eat with knives; forget the dessert, but have one ready to serve after volleyball. Plan volleyball and pretend to forget the ball. Really ham it up and have fun. Observe how the picnic works out, then discuss what happens when people don't follow through on their assignments. Explain how this shows what happens in a family when everyone doesn't do their part.

HOME SWEET HOME IDEAS:

Have young women bring several ideas that have made their home a pleasant place to live. Have them tell when they feel most comfortable at home, how they feel when the house is in order and clean, what they do when a guest is coming, how they feel when the guest arrives. Talk about home neglect: sweeping the dirt under the rug, piling junk in cupboards, closets, and drawers, leaving things out, clutter, and dirty dishes. Discuss strategies for keeping the home in order and what they can do to share their support and love. *Before You Start:* Prepare a bag with dirty laundry, smelly socks, and sweaty gym clothes. Have young women close their eyes while they smell the contents. Then have them close their eyes and smell a bag of clean clothes (dried on the clothesline or with air freshener sprayed inside). Talk about the odors that come from a dirty house and the clean smell that comes from a clean house. Share some "home sweet home" ideas.

TEACH A FILING SYSTEM:

Ask someone who is well organized to show young women how to file papers and notes that are worth keeping so they can find them quickly. *Ideas:* File Personal Progress planners, young women handouts, homework, family home evening lessons, bills, banking records, scrapbook photos and keepsakes in folders or in a notebook. To create a notebook filing system, place divider pockets inside a looseleaf notebook. Label the pockets with post-it-notes to name the subject or contents. Then slip the papers in the pockets to file and find quickly. Subjects might include: goals, money/savings, reading, family activities, friends, letters, or the other subjects (see the *Ideas* above).

HOME "TWEET" HOME NO-MESS NEST ROUTINE:

To Make: Print the pattern (shown right) from the *Personal Progress* CD-ROM*. Or, copy or print the pattern from the *Young Women Fun-tastic! Activities – Manual 2* book or CD-ROM (Lesson #6). *Color and cut out wheel parts A and B and put together placing a paper fastener (metal brad) in the center so bird turns. *Activity:* Create a *Home "Tweet" Home No-Mess Nest Routine* to help young women plan housework they wish to complete each day to make their home a pleasant place to live. Write tasks in pencil that you wish to complete each day. Try the routine for 21 days and you will develop the habit. *Daily Tasks to Maintain a High Quality of Life at Home:* cleaning their room, wiping down the shower and bathroom sink, making their bed, washing the dishes, sweeping the kitchen floor, taking out the garbage, etc.

*All images shown in this book can be printed in color or black and white from the
Young Women Fun-tastic! Personal Progress Motivators CD-ROM.

TIMER TACTICS:

Have young women go through a home with a timer in hand. Divide into pairs and assign a room, giving 5-10 minutes per room. Ask them to beat the clock and clean the room before the timer rings. With two working together, it makes work enjoyable and they can get twice as much done. Explain to them how much a little help around the house from every family member can make a big difference.

CLOSET CONCENTRATION:

Tell young women that next week they are going to have a closet tour, to get ready for inspection, and offer ideas on how to keep a closet clean. If they are not ready for the closet tour, others can come and help. *Ideas:* Hang clothes in groups of colors or items, hang empty hangers in front, drawers neat, simplify wardrobe, and have everything in its place.

BITING YOUR TONGUE:

Tell young women that learning to "bite their tongue" (not speak unkind words) begins at home. Ask young women, "Is this true or false? *'Sticks and stones will break my bones, but words will never hurt me.'*" Give each young woman a twig with this saying printed on an attached tag. Find poetry or an article about biting words that hurt. Talk about the term *"bite your tongue,"* and what it means. Discuss the short-term and long-term consequences of not biting our tongues when we need to. Discuss situations that may come up with family and friends, and what you might say in place of hurtful words.

SOAR HIGH! FAMILY COMMUNICATION BALLOON BOUQUET:

To Make: Print the patterns (shown left) from the *Personal Progress* CD-ROM*. Or, copy or print the patterns from the *Young Women Fun-tastic! Activities – Manual 2* book or CD-ROM (Lesson #8). *Color and tape images on a poster. Tie a string from each balloon and tie into a bouquet at the bottom.

Activity: Make a *Soar High!* balloon bouquet to help young women learn eight ways they can improve their family communication. Make and display a balloon bouquet on a poster. Have young women make one to share with their family and display in their room.

*All images shown in this book can be printed in color or black and white from the
Young Women Fun-tastic! Personal Progress Motivators CD-ROM.

20

COMPARE LASTING FAMILY RELATIONSHIPS WITH FADING FRIENDS:

Talk about getting along with your family now because family relationships are those that last. Bring pictures from your childhood (e.g., you in kindergarten, grade school, junior high, high school, your best friend in high school, or college, your boyfriends). As you show them, you might say, "I'm not as close to them now as I once was. The people who really matter now are my family, but at the time I gave up spending time with them to be with these short-term relationships." Give young women some time and stationery to write a long overdue note of appreciation to a family member.

EVENING OF SOAR HIGH! COMMUNICATION TECHNIQUES:

Have training on proper introductions, etiquette, and appropriate behavior (e.g., when to speak and not to speak). Have quotes and scriptures on communication (see James 1:26 and 3:5-6). Finish by playing Charades with phrases that go along with the lesson or some other similar game.
Ideas: "Be sure brain is engaged before putting mouth in gear." The best conversationalist focuses on the person they are talking to (mind off self is the secret of charm).

FAMILY COMMUNICATION SPEAKER(S):

Have someone talk about family communication. Look for someone who has a large family or someone the Relief Society or bishopric recommends. Find quotes from a family relations class that are appropriate and have the young women take turns sharing them. Or have a panel of two families and ask them questions.

WHOLESOME HOME:

Talk about having wholesome pictures, books, and music to create peace and love in the home. Show several of these and have them on display.

HARMONY IN THE HOME PANEL:

Have the bishopric and their wives do a panel discussion on harmony in their homes. Have each young woman write a question or two for discussion. (You could ask the stake presidency and wives to come also.) Have the girls record some of the things they learned or especially liked from the panel and discuss these ideas.

GOOD APPLE ATTITUDE POSTER:

To Make: Print the pattern (shown right) from the *Personal Progress* CD-ROM*. Or, copy or print the pattern from the *Young Women Fun-tastic! Activities – Manual 1* book or CD-ROM (Lesson #12). *Color.

Activity: Using this *Good Apple Attitudes* poster, talk about attitudes or actions that can spoil family relationships, and attitudes that can sweeten them. Encourage young women to use the poster to set goals with their family that will strengthen their family relationships. On each apple, write a family member's name and how you will strengthen your relationship with that person.

*All images shown in this book can be printed in color or black and white from the
Young Women Fun-tastic! Personal Progress Motivators CD-ROM.

21

PLANTING POSITIVE SEEDS:

Give young women dehydrated or fresh apples. As you eat the apples, talk about the seeds found in each one. One seed can create an apple tree, just as one thought or attitude can create a positive or negative atmosphere in the home. We can plant the seeds of kindness, happiness, patience, love, and respect each day. During this activity you could show them how to dehydrate apples and other fruit, such as kiwis, bananas, peaches, apricots.

DIVINE NATURE
— VALUE EXPERIENCE #4 TAKE UPON THE NAME OF JESUS CHRIST

SACRAMENT THOUGHT CARD:

To Make: Print the pattern (shown left) from the *Personal Progress* CD-ROM*. Or, copy or print the pattern from the *Young Women Fun-tastic! Activities - Manual 2* book or CD-ROM (Lesson #26). *Color, cut out, and glue cards back-to-back.

Activity: Give each young woman an *I Stand all Amazed* scripture card and read the 3 Nephi 11:14 scripture and Doctrine and Covenants 20:75 and Mosiah 5:7 to learn of actions that help you grow closer to the Savior. Then use the other side of this card to have young women write their feelings and thoughts of Jesus Christ. They could enclose this in their scriptures to pull out and ponder during the sacrament.

LAST SUPPER:

1. Create a setting like the Last Supper. Have the young women sit around a large table.
2. Discuss with them what went on at the Last Supper before Jesus was crucified.
3. Explain that Jesus wanted his disciples and us to always remember him and to keep his commandments.
4. Review the sacrament prayers found in the Book of Mormon (3 Nephi 18:7, 11).
5. Have someone who is particularly appreciative of the sacrament express his or her feelings about this sacred ordinance, and discuss a conference talk about the sacrament.
6. Use unleavened bread (or pita bread) to show what bread was like in the Savior's day.
7. Have everyone bring their scriptures to have a Sacrament Scripture Chase. Divide into two teams and race to find scriptures on the following. Announcing subject matter first, then the scripture. *Scripture Discussion:* Have the person who finds the scripture first read the scripture and discuss what it means to her.

Ideas: ✿ Priesthood ordinance (3 Nephi 18:15) ✿ Sacrament given to the Nephites after Christ's resurrection (3 Nephi 18:1-12) ✿ Importance of taking the sacrament each Sunday in sacrament

*All images shown in this book can be printed in color or black and white from the
Young Women Fun-tastic! Personal Progress Motivators CD-ROM.

22

meeting (D&C 20:75) ❀ Reminder of baptismal promises (D&C 20:37, Mosiah 18:6-10) ❀ Helps us think of Jesus and find peace (D&C 19:23-24) ❀ Reminds us that Jesus took our sins upon Him (Hebrews 9:28; 13:12, Mosiah 3:5-8) ❀ Jesus is the gate through which we enter heaven (John 14:6, 2 Nephi 9:41)

DIVINE NATURE — VALUE EXPERIENCE #5 STRIVE TO OBEY PARENTS

OBEDIENCE AND DISOBEDIENCE COOKIES:
1. Make Some Obedience Cookies. Choose a terrific cookie recipe and make it with the young women. Follow the recipe exactly and bake.
2. Make Some Disobedience Cookies. With the same recipe omit the sugar and salt or the baking soda or half the flavoring or sweet ingredients, e.g., vanilla, or chocolate chips. Bake and keep separate from the Obedience Cookies (above).
3. Discuss the Difference. Have a discussion around the table with milk and one each of the Obedience Cookies and Disobedience Cookies. Talk about what can happen in life if you choose not to obey certain commandments. Life can be sweet and full, or it may lack certain wonderful ingredients. As the Spirit directs, choose some scriptures to make the point. Bear testimony.

DIVINE NATURE — VALUE EXPERIENCE #6 DEVELOP DIVINE QUALITIES

❀ *Divine Quality: Chastity*
See also Choice and Accountability — Value Experience #6

❀ *Divine Quality: Honesty*

I'M "SEW" HONEST! STAND-UP CARD:
To Make: Print the pattern (shown right) from the *Personal Progress* CD-ROM*. Or, copy or print the pattern from the *Young Women Fun-tastic! Activities – Manual 2* book or CD-ROM (Lesson #36). *Color, cut out, and fold card to stand up.
Activity: Have young women write the blessings they receive from being honest on the *I'm Sew Honest* card. *Ideas:* Peace of mind, self-respect, others trust you, you don't have to remember what you said or did, you have a clear conscience and are not burdened with guilt.

In honesty, I measure up!
The blessings I receive from being honest are:

*All images shown in this book can be printed in color or black and white from the *Young Women Fun-tastic! Personal Progress Motivators* CD-ROM.

MALT SHOP HONESTY TEST:

Treat young women to a malt or milkshake. Tell the owner or cashier ahead of time that you are teaching a lesson on honesty. Have them charge you for one less item (e.g., seven malts when eight malts were served). Pay for your order, then check the bill after you leave. Tell the girls they made a mistake and only charged you for seven. Some will suggest going back to pay, some may say it's not worth the trouble. Then go back and make up the difference. Discuss why it was important to go back and pay.

HONEST REFLECTION:

Ask girls to think about who's cheating who when we are dishonest?

Step #1: Show a thin piece of fabric and talk about the veil that separates us from heaven. We have to live by faith, not seeing on the other side of the veil, but Heavenly Father knows our every thought and action. He knows the truth of all the things we think and do.

Step #2: Ask young women to quietly reflect on their past thoughts and actions regarding honesty at home, school, and in the community. Ask them to think: Do I cheat? Do I steal? Do I gossip?

Step #3: Discuss types of honesty. Some people don't feel it is dishonest when they copy a video that says no copying allowed or copy a song or a computer program; when they gossip or say they will call a friend when they don't intend to; they accept a date even though they aren't sixteen yet; they say they are older than they are; they accept a date when they aren't really interested in the boy; they say they paid a fine and they didn't, they steal another person's time by being late.

Step #4: Talk about feelings you have when you are dishonest. Say that honesty builds strength, and dishonesty breeds mistrust of others, dislike of self, feelings of sadness.

ARE YOU MISS HONEST OR DISHONEST? CONSEQUENCES JOURNAL:

To Make: Print the pattern (shown left) from the *Personal Progress* CD-ROM*. Or, copy or print the pattern from the *Young Women Fun-tastic! Activities – Manual 3* book or CD-ROM (Lesson #34). *Color.

Activity: Help the young women decide if they are *Miss Honest* or *Dishonest* with this *Consequences Journal*. This helps them think about the consequences of honest and dishonest choices. Ask them to honestly consider how these actions will affect their life by writing in detail the consequences for each decision. Example: The consequence for stealing is that people won't trust you.

❀ *Divine Quality: Prayer*

PRAYER AND SCRIPTURE REMINDERS:

Prayer rocks and angel pillow cases can remind young women to read their scriptures and say their prayers each morning and night. Place rock under pillow with the scriptures Nearby. *Prayer Rock Craft:* Create a prayer rock with the following verse attached: *To help you remember to say your prayers, place this rock under your pillow. If you get quickly in your bed and feel this rock hit your head, kneel down and pray and thank Heavenly Father for your day. Ask him for help in all you do and know of his great love for you.*

*All images shown in this book can be printed in color or black and white from the
Young Women Fun-tastic! Personal Progress Motivators CD-ROM.

24

COUNSEL WITH THE LORD TENT CARD/PRAYER CHART:

To Make: Print the pattern (shown right) from the *Personal Progress* CD-ROM*. Or, copy or print the pattern from the *Young Women Fun-tastic! Activities – Manual 2* book or CD-ROM (Lesson #22). *Color and cut out, cutting out the girl at the top, and fold card to stand up.

Activity: Give each young woman a *Counsel with the Lord* tent card to encourage them to make a greater effort to draw close to Heavenly Father through prayer. Read Alma 37:37 and talk about how we can *"counsel with the Lord in all [our] doings."* Have each girl write on the card how she can pray and what to pray for. On the flip side of the card, have her record for the next thirty days each time they say their morning and night prayers, filling in the box for each day.

DIVINE NATURE — VALUE EXPERIENCE #7: BE A PEACEMAKER

HOME IS HEAVENLY PEACEMAKER TENT CARD:

To Make: Print the pattern (shown right) from the *Personal Progress* CD-ROM*. Or, copy or print the pattern from the *Young Women Fun-tastic! Activities – Manual 2* book or CD-ROM (Lesson #9). *Color, cut out, and fold card to stand up.

Activity: Give each young woman a *Home is Heavenly When I'm a Peacemaker* tent card. Divide them into five groups, pairing off in two or more to talk privately about how each can be a peacemaker in these five areas (shown on the tent card, e.g., "I am a peacemaker because I show love and understanding"). Assign each group one of these areas to report on. Give each group five minutes and ask each to report how she plans to use this idea to be a peace-maker, e.g., "I will listen to my brother as he tells me about his day".

PEACEMAKER HINTS:

Have someone come and talk about ways to bring peace in the home.

Ideas: Learning relaxation techniques; creating peace when there is conflict; creating cooperation in the home; creating love when conflict comes; planning for and fixing meals ahead so that family members can eat on time; feeding the family spiritually; having scripture study, family home evening, and family counsel; planning family activities that bring peace and love; and sharing tasks.

PEACEFUL PUZZLE:

Encourage young women to think about developing peace within as they create a puzzle with pictures drawn of peaceful actions, or as they read the following quotes to remind them to develop good habits that bring feelings of peace. "*The chains of habit are generally too small to be felt until they are too strong to be broken.*" (Samuel Johnson) "*Better keep yourself clean and bright; you are the window through which you must see the world.*" (George Bernard Shaw)

*All images shown in this book can be printed in color or black and white from the *Young Women Fun-tastic! Personal Progress Motivators* CD-ROM.

25

PEACEMAKER PEBBLE:

Give each young woman a pebble with the following note and challenge them to be a peacemaker, helping her entire family to feel peace when she is around.

PEBBLE PROMISE: "This week I will look at this pebble and remember to be a peacemaker. When a pebble is tossed into a pool of water, it creates a ripple, making larger and larger circles, showing how this one pebble's influence is widespread. My one action of being a peacemaker can affect my entire family. I will be a peacemaker."

ROSE-COLORED DAY:

Tell young women that having joy in their day is all in the way they look at it. You can look at your day with rose colored glasses or dark glasses. Looking on the bright side requires 15-second thought changes when things don't look bright. For example, when studying for a test, talking to someone you don't know well, or cleaning your room or the bathroom, take the first 5 seconds to decide that you want a better attitude, the next 5 seconds to decide on the attitude, and the next 5 seconds to repeat that positive attitude.

Joy-less Thoughts: "I hate this." "I'd rather be watching TV." "They don't like me."

Joy-ful Thoughts: "This will bring my mom happiness." "It will feel good to have this clean." "Someday I will use this in college or to teach my future child." "I will invite her to go."

GO WITH POSITIVE MOTTOS EACH DAY:

Show traffic signs and talk about actions young women wish to STOP and actions they wish to GO with to make their environment uplifting. They have the power to create happiness each day as they choose positive mottos to live by.

Ideas to copy onto cardstock paper so young women can post on their mirror:

❀ If it is to be, it is up to me.
❀ Greet the day with a song.
❀ Practice smiling three times a day.
❀ Take my mind off myself to focus on others.
❀ Make my room, home, or work place clean and inviting.
❀ Create a house of order, a house of prayer.
❀ Feed my spirit daily with the scriptures, Church books, magazines, and song.
❀ Pray daily to invite the Spirit.
❀ Look for the good in others.
❀ An interesting person talks to others about their interests.
❀ Share positive thoughts and feelings.
❀ Don't attend every argument you're invited to.
❀ Work ahead so as not to lose your head.
❀ Cook up a storm, but don't let the dishes reign.

*All images shown in this book can be printed in color or black and white from the
Young Women Fun-tastic! Personal Progress Motivators CD-ROM.

26

Please come to a Personal Progress activity!

Date: _____

Time: _____

Place: _____

Bring: _____

Your Divine Nature Can Really Shine Through

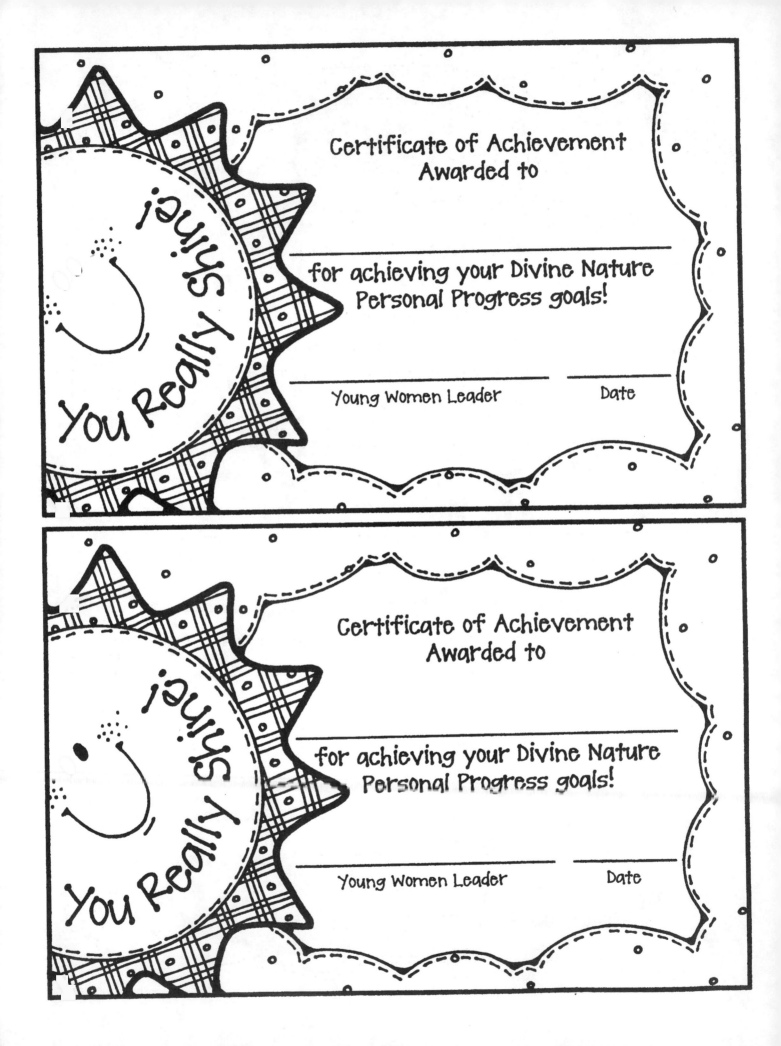

You Really Shine!

Certificate of Achievement
Awarded to

_____

for achieving your Divine Nature
Personal Progress goals!

_____   _____

Young Women Leader   Date

You Really Shine!

Certificate of Achievement
Awarded to

_____

for achieving your Divine Nature
Personal Progress goals!

_____   _____

Young Women Leader   Date

Discover and Build Upon Divine Qualities as You Are a Daughter of God

Divine Nature – Value Experience #1:

SEARCH AND PONDER:

2 Peter 1, Alma 7:23-24, and Doctrine and Covenants 121:45

"The Family: A Proclamation to the World"

(see Personal Progress Book, page ii).

Divine Qualities Discussed in My Reading:

_____

_____

_____

_____

How I Can Discover and Build upon Each of These Qualities:

_____

_____

_____

_____

_____

_____

_____

_____

_____

_____

Look Forward to Quality Womanhood

Divine Nature – Value Experience #2:

SEARCH AND PONDER:

Proverbs 31:10-31

"The Family: A Proclamation to the World"

(see Personal Progress Book, page ii)

After Reading Two Conference Talks on Womanhood, this Is
What I Discovered about a Quality Wife and Mother:

Talk #1: _____ by: _____

_____

_____

Talk #2: _____ by: _____

_____

_____

After Asking a Mother What She Thinks Are Important
Attributes for Being a Mother, I Discovered:

_____

_____

I Worked to Develop the Following Attributes:

_____

For Two Weeks: __ Week #1 __ Week #2

My Successes:

_____

Make Home Life Better

Divine Nature – Value Experience #3:

For Two Weeks I Made a Special Effort to Strengthen My Relationship With a Family Member by Showing Love.

Family Member(s): _____

_____ I did not criticize: _____

_____

_____ I did not speak unkindly: _____

_____

_____ I watched for positive qualities in that person: _____

_____

_____ I wrote notes to encourage this person: _____

_____

_____ I prayed for this family member: _____

_____

_____ I found ways to be helpful: _____

_____

_____ I found ways to verbally express my love: _____

_____

Week #1: M ___ T ___ W ___ T ___ F ___ S ___ S ___

Week #2: M ___ T ___ W ___ T ___ F ___ S ___ S ___

Take Upon the Name of Jesus Christ

Divine Nature – Value Experience #4:

During the Sacrament I Listened Carefully to the
Prayers and Thought About:
What it Means to Take upon the Name of Jesus Christ:

_____

_____

How Doing this Affects My Actions and Decisions:

_____

_____

I Practiced Keeping My Baptismal Covenants
By Doing Something Each Day to Help Me
Remember the Lord Jesus Christ (For Two Weeks):

Week #1: M __ T __ W __ T __ F __ S __ S __

Week #2: M __ T __ W __ T __ F __ S __ S __

These Are the Things I Did to Follow Jesus:

_____

_____

_____

Strive to Obey Parents

Divine Nature – Value Experience #5:

SEARCH AND PONDER:

Luke 2:40-51

I Made a Special Effort to Do What My Parents
Asked Me to Do Without Being Reminded for Two Weeks:

Week #1: M __ T __ W __ T __ F __ S __ S __

Week #2: M __ T __ W __ T __ F __ S __ S __

How Being More Obedient to My Parents
Motivated Me to Want to Continue to Obey:

_____

_____

_____

_____

_____

_____

_____

_____

Develop Divine Qualities

Divine Nature – Value Experience #6:

SEARCH AND PONDER:

Matthew 5:9, John 15:12, Galatians 5:22-23,
Colossians 3:12-17, 1 John 15:12, and Moroni 7:44-48

I Identified These Divine Qualities in the above Scriptures:

_____

_____

_____

_____

I Memorized My Favorite Verse from the above Scriptures:

_____

_____

I Selected One Quality: _____

And Made it a Part of My Daily Life for Two Weeks:

Week #1: M ___ T ___ W ___ T ___ F ___ S ___ S ___

Week #2: M ___ T ___ W ___ T ___ F ___ S ___ S ___

My Experiences:

_____

_____

_____

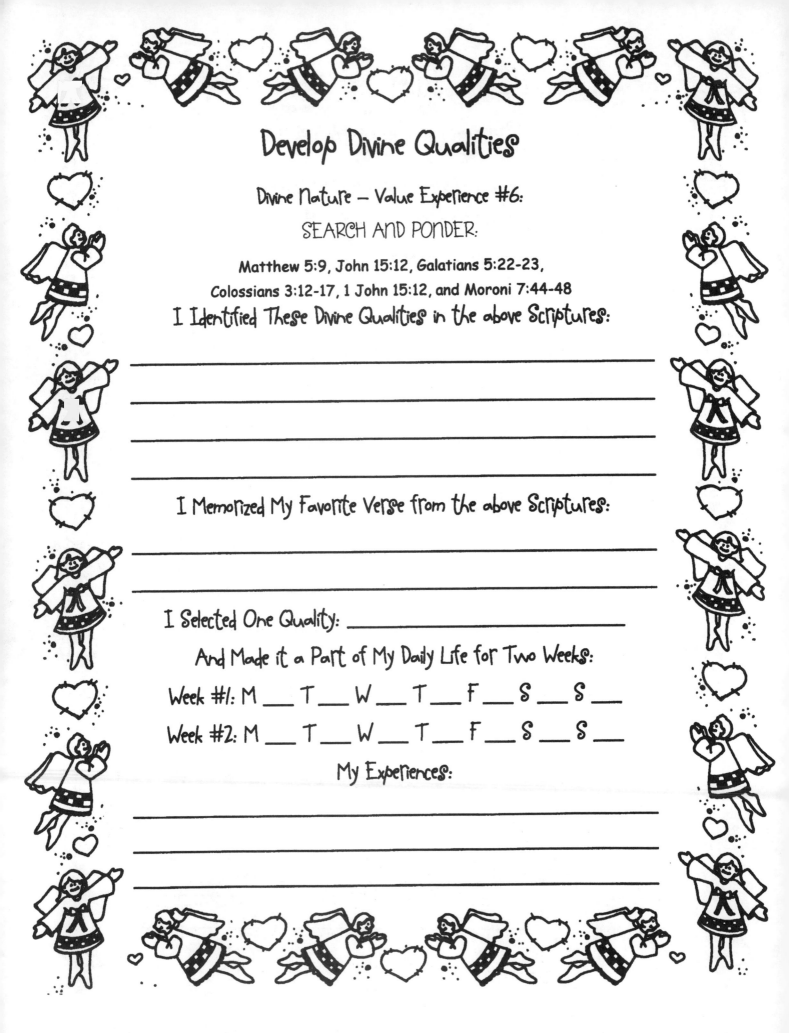

Let your light so shine!

Become a Peacemaker

Divine Nature — Value Experience #7:

Definition of Peacemaker: _____

_____

_____

Five Scriptures that Teach about Peacemakers:

SCRIPTURES: What they Teach About Peace:

#1: _____

_____

#2: _____

_____

#3: _____

_____

#4: _____

_____

#5: _____

_____

____ I tried to be a peacemaker a home by not criticizing, complaining, or speaking unkindly to or about others.

____ I prayed morning and evening for help to do the above:

Week #1: M __ T __ W __ T __ F __ S __ S __

Week #2: M __ T __ W __ T __ F __ S __ S __

Divine Nature Value Project Planner

My Project Is:

_____

_____

_____

Steps to Carry Out My Project:

1. _____
2. _____
3. _____
4. _____
5. _____
6. _____
7. _____
8. _____

How I Felt about the Project:

_____

_____

How My Understanding of Divine Nature Increased with this Project:

_____

_____

_____

Midweek Motivational Activities:
Value: Individual Worth
Theme: We Have a Divine Mission to Fulfill

Invitation and Certificates: (1) *Copy the invitation and
certificate (p. 50) for each young woman. (2) *Color and cut out
images and fill in details. (3) To make invitation, pierce holes in
diamond and insert raffia, tying on the "price" tag. Glue back to
back. Deliver a week ahead. (4) See #5 below (certificate).

Goal Planning and Sharing: You'll need a *copy of the
Individual Worth Value Experience #1-7 planners and the Individual Worth Value Project Planner
(pages 51-58) for each young woman.

DISTRIBUTE FORMS AND HAVE ONE OR MORE ACTIVITIES
FROM THE FOLLOWING PAGES "FUN WAYS TO TEACH VALUES":

1. Tell young women that they are of
infinite worth with their own divine
mission they can fulfill. Read Doctrine and
Covenants 18:10 (shown on page 26 in the
Personal Progress booklet).

2. Give each young woman a set of
Individual Worth Value Experience #1-7
planners and a Value Project Planner
(sample shown left). Review each planner
#1-7 titles, e.g., #1: "*You Are a Daughter
of Heavenly Father Who Loves You.*"

3. Suggest that they use the planners as
worksheets to plan and carry out their
goals and as a journal to record their
experiences. When young women have passed off their goals,
they can record these in their Personal Progress journal, if
desired.

4. Suggest that they post the planners on the
mirror as a reminder. When complete, store them in
a looseleaf notebook or folder (see Introduction).

5. Award an Individual Worth certificate and a quilt
block to young women who have achieved all their
IW goals. See the Appendix to make the quilt.

*All images shown in this book can be printed in color or black and white from the
Young Women Fun-tastic! Personal Progress Motivators CD-ROM.

Fun Ways to Teach Values:

Choose one or more of the following activities to motivate goal achievement.

Individual Worth — VALUE EXPERIENCE #1: DAUGHTER OF GOD

VALUABLE MIRROR REFLECTIONS:
1. Have young women go into a room where they can look into a large mirror or you can give each one a hand mirror. Ask them to really look at themselves and to smile.
2. Ask them to take another look in the mirror this next week and talk to themselves about their potential. Ask them to smile and tell themselves that they are daughters of Heavenly Father and that they are of great worth and value. Tell them that if they do this day after day then one day they will come to believe that they are truly daughters of God and that they are deeply loved. This realization will help them have true joy.

PATRIARCHAL BLESSING DISCUSSION AND SACRED YEARLY LETTER:
1. Talk about patriarchal blessings and about earthly fathers—what they want for their children and what they do for their children. Discuss what Heavenly Father does and wants for his children, and things he gives us to help us.
2. Have young women write a letter of appreciation to their Heavenly Father and put it in a sealed envelope. Tell them to nourish these feelings so they will grow. Have them put the letter in their journal for one year.
3. After the year waiting period is up, have them then write another letter to Heavenly Father, expressing appreciation and love, then read the letter from the last year.
4. Repeat steps 2-3 and compare the feelings from one year to the next. Each year they can see their love grow as they read their thoughts and see them increase in love.

SEND A LETTER HOME:
Give each young woman a helium balloon and ask her to take the balloon home. When she is alone, she can write a note to Heavenly Father on the balloon with a marker, sharing her gratitude for what he has done and listing her personal goals. After she signs it, she can let it go soaring toward heaven.

ROYALTY PROCESSION:
Invite parents to enjoy this evening with the young women. The purpose is to honor young women for their desire to obey the commandments and obtain the celestial kingdom.
❀ *Before Activity:*
1. Decorate the room by rolling out red carpet (red butcher paper). Place red paper carpet in the center aisle between the chairs where the parents are seated.
2. Outline the commandments we are asked to live in order to become queens in the celestial kingdom.
3. Create a 10" x 5" royalty bandelo for each young woman that streams over their right shoulder and over their back. Start by cutting several bandelos out of colored paper (use a variety of

colors). On each bandelo write a commandments, e.g, "Honor Parents."

4. Make up a script for each young woman to read. The script would tell about the commandment she is representing, e.g., *I am of royal blood, a princess in Heavenly Father's kingdom. I will honor my parents. I will seek for their guidance. I will listen to their counsel as they guide me in righteousness.*

❀ *During the Activity:*

1. Have each young woman take turns walking up the red paper carpet and reading her script.

2. Place a crown on her head and give her a silk flower that represents one of the values.

Individual Worth — VALUE EXPERIENCE #2: PLAN AND PREPARE

MY ANT FARM LEISURE TIME LOG:

To Make: Print the pattern (shown right) from the *Personal Progress* CD-ROM*. Or, copy or print the pattern from the *Young Women Fun-tastic! Activities – Manual 2* book or CD-ROM (Lesson #43). *Color.

Activity: Give each young woman a *My Ant Farm Leisure Time Log* and tell them: "Eternity is won or lost in our leisure time."

Ask them to record on the *Time Log* activities they can do in their free time which are a wise use of time. (1) Study the ideas found on this log. (2) Have young women circle activities they want to do in their free time, adding activities to the list. (3) Encourage them to schedule chosen activities during their free time. This way they will have something to do during their free time, and they will have something to look forward to each day. (4) Talk about "dovetailing" activities. Dovetailing is doing two things at once to save time to save time. Examples: washing the dishes and studying your notes for a test, manicure your nails while you talk to friends on the phone. Read, exercise, or drink water during television advertisements. Eat an apple while you do your homework. Listen to uplifting music or a motivational tape as you clean.

THE BRICK PATH GAME:

The objective is help young women understand that life has its challenges and they need to rely on others to help them achieve their goals safely and completely.

Items Needed: Parking lot or driveway, table and cloth, treats, chalk, six bricks or more depending on how many young women are participating (have one more brick than the number of girls).

To Set Up: Place the table at some designated spot. You could place some labeled treats, e.g., "celestial cinnamon rolls" or "career cookies" and milk on a table at this spot. This represents the desired goals. Draw a line several feet in front of the table and mark it "the goal line." Approximately 20-30 feet away from the goal line, place five bricks on the pavement perpendicular to the goal line.

To Play:

1. Have five young women stand on the five bricks. Place the sixth brick behind the last girl. She is responsible to pick up the brick and pass it to the girl in front of her who in turn passes it to the girl in front of her and so on. When the girl closest to the goal gets the brick, she is to put it down in front of herself and steps on it. The girls all then step up, leaving the last brick vacant which starts the process over again until they all get past the goal line and celebrate their achievement.

2. When you have finished this activity and are sitting and enjoying the treats (sweet rewards of success), ask the girls questions such as: ❀ "What did you discover about yourself?" ❀ "What did you discover about your friends?" ❀ "What are the advantages of working as a team (friends); with help (guides, mentors, leaders)?" ❀ "Could you do this alone?" ❀ "How hard would it be doing it alone?" ❀ "What are the dangers of doing it alone?" (When you start falling, there is no one there to help steady you.) ❀ "Are there any advantages in doing it alone?" ❀ "How does our Father in Heaven and Savior want us to go through life?" ❀ "What have they provided us with to help us?"

3. You will be inspired to ask questions. If the girls have really given it a lot of thought, they will discover things about themselves and their friends. They will look at life's path a little differently. As a leader, do not give them the answers; let them think. There may be moments of silence, but that means they are pondering, weighing and considering, and hopefully connecting with the Spirit. At the end of this activity you could ask them to think of some of their most favorite guides and friends. These could be parents, Christ, bishops, mentors, leaders, special friends, etc.

4. Prior to the activity, go over it in your mind and see it happening. Allow the Spirit to define the activity and its goals. As you think about the activity, apply it to your own life. You will think of additional questions to ask the girls and perhaps even be inspired to share an experience from your past that could help them more fully understand the importance of guides and good friends in their lives.

MY FUTURE LOOKS BRIGHT GOAL PLANNER:

To Make: Print the pattern (shown left) from the *Personal Progress* CD-ROM*. Or, copy or print the pattern from the *Young Women Fun-tastic! Activities – Manual 1* (Lesson #48) book or CD-ROM. *Color.

Activity: Ask young women to use the *My Future Looks Bright Goal Planner* to choose a goal and using the six steps, make short-range goals that help them achieve success! Help young women realize that their future looks bright as they plan for a sparkling life. With this form they can project what they want to be and what they want to do.

GOAL ANTICIPATION EXERCISES:

Have young women think of ways they can anticipate their future, looking forward to the next goal.

1. They can make an "anticipation poster" with a long-range goal and begin collecting pictures that remind them of their goal (e.g., for a trip to Hawaii, they can collect brochures, find pictures of

*All images shown in this book can be printed in color or black and white from the
Young Women Fun-tastic! Personal Progress Motivators CD-ROM.

40

tropical treats and a girl in a bathing suit, even place sand in a bag and attach to poster to anticipate the sand on the beach). Have them write their goal on the poster, when they plan to finish, and the steps needed to achieve their goal.

2. Give each young woman a "goal/project" notebook she can use to list long-range goals and projects (one on each page). Encourage young women to fill the book, then make a numerical or A-Z contents or index to cross-reference the goal or project.

SUCCESS SEMINAR:

Have different speakers who are experts in one skill or another train young women to live in this world of competition, and live with honor. Have them talk about treating others with respect as girls pursue their education and career both inside and outside the home. Talk about how to organize and make the best use of their time. Have speakers tell how they use success tools such as a planner, phone, computer, and office equipment to succeed. Some could talk about successful home careers and the advantages of working at home. They could also talk about the skills needed to work at home.

TIME IN A BOTTLE SPIN-THE-BOTTLE:

Have young women sit in a circle with a bottle in the center full of time hints (see below). Take turns spinning the bottle. The person it points to opens the bottle, takes out a time hint and reads it aloud. Share how this time hint could help you use your time wisely. Place the following hints in bottle. Copy hints for young women to take home.

Time Hints: ☺ Retire and rise early. ☺ There's a difference between leisure and lazy. ☺ Prioritize tasks to get the most out of your day. ☺ Plan time or others will control your time. ☺ If not 10 minutes early, you're 10 minutes late. ☺ Don't waste your time. Spot actions that are time wasters. ☺ Don't let TV rob your time. ☺ Give time to important tasks first when you have energy. ☺ Make a list and check it twice. ☺ Think of your planner as your brain book. ☺ Take care of your health, giving you energy to use your time wisely. ☺ Pray daily before planning your time. ☺ If at first you don't succeed, reschedule. ☺ Goals are only dreams until they are written. ☺ Each day can be the start of a bright future. ☺ Schedule scripture time to lighten your day. ☺ Time is a tool that only you can work.

LEISURE PICNIC TO TALK ABOUT LEISURE TIME:

Have a picnic indoors or outdoors. Call ahead and ask every young woman and leader bring: (1) a sack lunch, (2) a blanket, and (3) ideas to share of leisure-time productive activities and leisure-time time-wasting activities. Decorate by enlarging drawings of ants and placing one on each blanket. Talk about industrious ants and how they don't waste their leisure time. Have a sharing time on what all the girls do. Have each young woman and the leaders stand up and share their ideas.

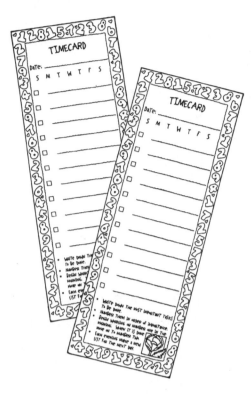

TIMECARD TO PRACTICE TIME MANAGEMENT:

To Make: Print the pattern (shown left) from the *Personal Progress* CD-ROM*. Or, copy or print the pattern from the *Young Women Fun-tastic! Activities – Manual 1* book or CD-ROM (Lesson #44). *Color.

Activity: Encourage young women to follow the advice of an efficiency expert by using the *Timecard* to write down the most important tasks to be performed each day for one week. Follow instructions on card. Review the following scriptures on time: Eccles. 3:1, 8:5, D&C 60:13, and 1 Nephi 15:32. Using a time card for each day of the week, write down and prioritize each task and check it off when complete. You may want to make several copies of the *Timecard* for each girl.

PLAN AHEAD:

Gather young women together and say you are making cookies. Do not bring the eggs. Have the young women go to someone's house close to the church and borrow eggs. If possible pre-arrange with a few people to not have the needed eggs. They can then direct young women to another house, perhaps next door. When they find eggs, begin to make the cookies, then say, "Oh, I forgot the milk." Ask young women to get the milk from a pre-assigned home. As you sit and eat cookies, talk about planning ahead, making lists, getting things done in order, etc. This could be quite fun if "planned" well.

TIME TRACKER JOURNAL:

To Make: Print the pattern (shown left) from the *Personal Progress* CD-ROM*. Or, copy or print the pattern from the *Young Women Fun-tastic! Activities – Manual 3* book or CD-ROM (Lesson #44). *Color.

Activity: Using this *Time Tracker* journal, encourage young women to manage their time and "not run faster or labor more than they have strength." Read Mosiah 4:27 and D&C 10:4 as found on the motivation poster *Time Tracker*. Help young women write on this journal ways they can: ❀ "Establish Priorities" ❀ "Eliminate Unimportant Things" ❀ "Improve Work and Study Habits" and ❀ "Recognize Limitations." Ask young women to try the above, using a calendar or planner and a clock or egg-timer to track their time daily.

*All images shown in this book can be printed in color or black and white from the
Young Women Fun-tastic! Personal Progress Motivators CD-ROM.

42

PLAN TO SUCCEED:

Ask young women and leaders to share their ideas on planning for success.

Ideas: ❀ Have a place for everything and have everything in its place. ❀ Give away things you don't absolutely need. ❀ Plan your day in detail with a calendar or planner. ❀ Allow time for flexibility (don't plan your schedule too tightly). ❀ Take care of priorities first. ❀ Plan time for your family and for service. ❀ Make checklists and check them often. ❀ Plan a healthy diet and exercise program. ❀ Plan self-time: relax, read, think. ❀ Pray and read the scriptures. ❀ Plan a weekly family home evening. ❀ Plan for a career (especially a home career). ❀ Plan and schedule goals and activities.

NOBLE CAREER: (See KNOWLEDGE VALUE EXPERIENCE #1: GAINING KNOWLEDGE)

STEPS TO CHOOSE CAREERS: (See KNOWLEDGE VALUE EXPERIENCE #1: GAINING KNOWLEDGE)

STUDY HABITS: (See KNOWLEDGE VALUE EXPERIENCE #1: GAINING KNOWLEDGE)

STRESS REDUCTION:

Ask young women and leaders to share their ideas on ways to reduce stress.

Ideas: ❀ Focus on your strengths and how they can help you in stressful times. ❀ Develop a sense of humor—cry, laugh. ❀ Take a break—walk in the fresh air. ❀ Exercise ❀ Listen to music you like. ❀ Talk to parents, family, and Heavenly Father about problems and really listen. ❀ Accept your school, home, church, and work responsibilities. ❀ Schedule priorities. ❀ Save for things you will need in the future. ❀ Plan your time. ❀ Change habits that cause stress. ❀ Eat healthfully, avoiding junk food.

Individual Worth — VALUE EXPERIENCE #3: BUILD OTHER'S SELF-WORTH

ATTITUDE ADJUSTMENT:

In this "put-down" world, do a "face-lift" activity. Have some moms come and pamper their daughters. If you can use a beauty salon (after hours), great; but if not, just make due by making a salon setting. Have moms wash their daughters' hair, do their nails, give a facial, neck massage, etc. Have each mother write a letter to their daughter ahead of time, expressing her belief in her, that she can make it through this world of ups and downs.

SUPER DAD AND MOM SPOTLIGHT:

To Make: Print the pattern (shown left) from the *Personal Progress* CD-ROM*. Or, copy or print the pattern from the *Young Women Fun-tastic! Activities – Manual 1* book or CD-ROM (Lesson #9). *Color.

Activity: Encourage young women to honor their parents using this *Super Dad and Mom Spotlight* form.

Option #1: Use form to spotlight parents and give positive highlights from their lives (or from their lives since the birth of the young woman). These could be read during an "Honor Parents" night.

Option #2: Use form to write a plan with brothers and sisters how they will express honor and appreciation to parents. Then carry out the plan.

Option #3: Use forms to write a letter of appreciation to parents.

Option #4: Use form to write personal goals to show honor and respect to parents. Then work on those goals.

PARENT APPRECIATION NIGHT:

1. The week before, have young women write a note to their parent(s) or guardian with at least four points of appreciation. Leaders could secretly tie each note (with parents' name on top) to a plastic fork with a ribbon. Leaders could also write a note to each young woman, expressing specific points of appreciation and attaching a fork (with name on note).

2. Young women invite their parents, grandparents, or guardian to a dinner.

3. Serve a spaghetti and salad dinner without eating utensils. Provide handy wipes to wipe hands before and after the meal.

4. After the meal, a leader says, "*Just like this fork [hold fork up], we often take many things for granted that our young women and parents do for us. Tonight we would like to honor our young women and parents, and express our points of appreciation (point to points on fork). Each young woman has prepared a note expressing their points of appreciation, and we the leaders have a note expressing our points of appreciation to our young women. Thank you. We will now serve dessert and you will be able to eat with your forks.*"

5. Pass out individualized forks with notes attached to each individual.

6. Serve dessert with a different fork.

7. Optional Favors: Place a flower on moms' plates and a Big Hunk candy bar on dads' plates.

*All images shown in this book can be printed in color or black and white from the *Young Women Fun-tastic! Personal Progress Motivators* CD-ROM.

44

Individual Worth — VALUE EXPERIENCE #4: PARTICIPATE IN A PERFORMANCE

See also Knowledge - Value Experience #2

I LOVE CULTURAL ARTS! FRAME:

To Make: Print the pattern (shown right) from the *Personal Progress CD-ROM**. Or, copy or print the pattern from the *Young Women Fun-tastic! Activities – Manual 2* book or CD-ROM (Lesson #45). *Color.

Activity: Have young women take a photo of themselves participating in a performance and place it inside this *I Love the Cultural Arts* frame to place in their scrapbooks. Or they can use this as a journal page to describe the performance.

More Ideas: Review the Thirteenth Article of Faith and ask young women to think of ways they can add to their life and to the lives of children through cultural arts. Many of these ideas are found in the frame/journal page. Have them refer to the pictures on the frame as they plan cultural arts activities. They could also save tickets and programs for special events to place in their journal.

PUT ON A PLAY FOR THE NEXT WARD PARTY.

TEACH DANCE STEPS: Have someone come and teach the basics: Ballet, western swing, line dancing, square dancing, folk dance, ballroom, disco, break dancing, and more.

Individual Worth — VALUE EXPERIENCE #5: FAMILY HISTORY

PORTRAIT OF MY ANCESTOR:

To Make: Print the pattern (shown right) from the *Personal Progress* CD-ROM*. Or, copy or print the pattern from the *Young Women Fun-tastic! Activities – Manual 2* book or CD-ROM (Lesson #17). *Color.

Activity: Encourage young women to go through their pedigree chart, learn about and write about their ancestors, and use the *Portrait of My Ancestor* form to write detailed information. Then share this with the other young women. Have them spotlight an ancestor using the *portrait* as a guide. Encourage them to photocopy a picture of their ancestor and reduce it to fit the page, or draw a picture/portrait of what they thought that their ancestor looked like. You may want to give the girls more than one copy of the *Portrait of My Ancestor* form so they can spotlight more ancestors. Encourage them to keep these with the pedigree charts in their notebooks.

*All images shown in this book can be printed in color or black and white from the *Young Women Fun-tastic! Personal Progress Motivators* CD-ROM.

45

FAMILY HISTORY LIBRARY NAME SEARCH:

Visit the Family History library and search for a name. Have each young woman find a name they would like to search, even if it's their own name. Have someone in the library take them through the research steps to find the name. Ask your ward family history representative for help.

FAITH-PROMOTING FAMILY HISTORY EXPERIENCES:

Ask someone who has been researching their family history to tell of their faith-promoting experiences as they've done family research, submitted names for temple work, and written their family history.

BAPTISMS FOR THE DEAD:

Inquire if someone in your ward needs work done for someone in their family. While at the temple, ask young women to pay attention to the dates and names that impressed them. Share your experiences afterward around a banana split or ice cream soda. Ask them how they think those deceased persons, for whom they were baptized, felt that day. Estimate the number of years they may have waited for this great day.

PLAN A PARTY AFTER BAPTISMS FOR THE DEAD:

Take young women to the temple to be baptized for the dead. Have a special dinner with promise placemats and packages. Talk about the promises we made at our baptism and the promises Heavenly Father makes us in return as we keep our baptismal covenants. Our Promises: to obey the commandments, read the scriptures, honor parents, help others, pay tithing, attend Church meetings. Heavenly Father's Promises: to forgive us when we repent, love and bless us, give us the gift of the Holy Ghost, answer prayers, let us live with Him forever.

FAMILY REUNION BRAINSTORM:

Have young women come with their ideas for food, fun, and games for a family reunion. Challenge young women to help their parents plan and organize a family reunion.

Ideas: Hide family photos; the first to find Grandpa Ross wins! Make cupcakes and hide Grandma Ross's name in one. Write her name on a small piece of paper and wrap it in tin foil. Bake it or slip it inside an already baked cupcake.

CLOSENESS CHECKLIST AND POSTCARD:

To Make: Print the patterns (shown left) from the *Personal Progress* CD-ROM*. Or, copy or print the patterns from the *Young Women Fun-tastic! Activities – Manual 3* book or CD-ROM (Lesson #11). Cut out.

ACTIVITY: Encourage young women to make time for extended family, to include them in their circle of love, remembering that families are forever. If they begin now to develop strong family ties, they will not be alone when they are separated from their immediate family. They will have someone they can call or communicate with when they are in need, and someone they can serve.

*All images shown in this book can be printed in color or black and white from the
Young Women Fun-tastic! Personal Progress Motivators CD-ROM.

Steps to Become Close: (1) Use the *I will be a friend to extended family,* checklist to plan what you will do to become close to that chosen family member. (2) Circle or highlight several things you wish to do in the following year to become close to that person. Schedule these actions on a calendar this week. (3) Begin by sending this extended family member a postcard. Decorate the front, write a quick note, and send it off this week!

GRAMMY AWARDS NIGHT:

Have young women create a potluck dinner for a grandmother or grandfather. Have them spotlight the grandparent and award them with a Grammy Award cookie or certificate or a Gramps Award cookie or certificate (for the grandfather).

"RELATIVE"-LY FUN NIGHT:

Create a fun night for young women to bring a parent or relative. Relatives can take turns sharing how they remember the young woman, spotlighting her for her kind deeds and warm ways.

ORGANIZE FAMILY GREETING CARDS:

Create greeting card storage pockets to store greeting cards months ahead to send to relatives. Young women can contact relatives to learn of their birthdays, and make homemade cards to send. *How to Create Pockets:* Cut an 8 ½" x 11" sheet of paper in half, width-wise. Glue the half sheet of paper to the bottom of an 8 ½" x 11" sheet of paper; placing glue on the sides and bottom, leaving the top open to insert greeting cards. Write a different month of the year on each pocket, e.g., January. Three-hole punch the pockets to place in young women's journals. Glue a 3" x 5" card on the front of pockets to write special dates to send greeting cards, e.g., holidays, birthdays, parents' anniversary. Create two more pockets to enclose thank-you and get-well cards.

FAMILY PHOTO SESSION:

Have young women bring some favorite family photos to show and tell about an extended family member. Ask them to tell one or two reasons why they love this extended family member, and share a fond experience or story about them. Remind them that as they extend their love to family members, they will create lasting memories they can share with their children.

MY TIME LINE STICKER JOURNAL:

To Make: Print the glue-on sticker patterns (shown right) from the *Personal Progress* CD-ROM*. Or, copy or print the patterns from the *Young Women Fun-tastic! Activities – Manual 1* book or CD-ROM (Lesson #19).
Activity: Use the glue-on stickers to:
Option #1: Create a Personal Time Line Journal.
Option #2: Create a Time Line Poster.
This will help young women map out their life's events and stories they wish to write in their journal. Have them *color and cut out images to create a poster to place in journal.

MAKE COVERED PHOTO ALBUMS AND DO SCRAPBOOKING:

Ideas: Cover a looseleaf binder with quilted fabric by cutting and gluing the outside cover, leaving a border folded over on the inside. Cut and glue the inside left and right pieces, folding inward so seams don't show. Have young women bring their scrapbooks and others with creative scrapbooks to share their ideas.

LEARN ABOUT YOUNG WOMEN:

Talk to parents to learn something special in the life of each young woman. Ask for a story about one of the young woman's ancestors (and supply a photo if possible). Then play *Guess Who? Ancestor and Story Match:* Put all the photos on the wall and have the young women match the ancestor to each young woman. Read some of the stories and see if anyone can guess whose relative it is. Ask parents for stories the young women don't know about their ancestors. Say, "These experiences are precious, and everything we learn about our ancestors helps us appreciate them more."

Individual Worth — VALUE EXPERIENCE #6: PATRIARCHAL BLESSINGS

PATRIARCHAL BLESSING PREP CHECKLIST AND MESSAGES MEMO:

To Make: Print the patterns (shown left) from the *Personal Progress* CD-ROM*. Or, copy or print the patterns from the *Young Women Fun-tastic! Activities - Manual 2* book or CD-ROM (Lesson #13). *Color.

Activity: Help young women prepare themselves for their patriarchal blessings by using the *Patriarchal Blessing Preparation Checklist.* After receiving their blessing, have them read their blessing with a prayerful heart and record the special messages on the *Patriarchal Blessing Messages Memo.* Encourage them to live worthy to receive the blessings promised.

PATRIARCH WIFE'S VIEW:

Have the wife of a patriarch come and relate her special insights and experiences regarding patriarchal blessings. She can also tell what she does to support her husband. Tell the steps involved in obtaining a patriarchal blessing, then tell what to do with your patriarchal blessing and how to read and understand it so it will help you throughout your life.

INSIGHTS OF LIVING A PATRIARCHAL BLESSING:

Have different mothers and older women in the ward who have received their patriarchal blessing share how it has helped them in their life. Discuss how each blessing is different and very personal. If parts of a blessing are shared, approve what is shared with leaders ahead of time.

*All images shown in this book can be printed in color or black and white from the
Young Women Fun-tastic! Personal Progress Motivators CD-ROM.*

48

Individual Worth — VALUE EXPERIENCE #7: SPECIAL GIFTS FROM HEAVENLY FATHER

SPIRITUAL GIFTS WRITING ACTIVITY AND MATCH GAME:

To Make: Print the pattern (shown right) from the *Personal Progress* CD-ROM*. Or, copy or print the pattern from the *Young Women Fun-tastic! Activities – Manual 2* book or CD-ROM (Lesson #2). *Color and cut out the gift envelope and cards. Fold the tabs and glue envelope together leaving the top flap open. Insert gift cards inside.

Activity: Tell young women there are two different kinds of gifts, tangible and intangible. Tangible gifts that come wrapped up in a package are nice, but they do not last long. If we focus on these gifts too much, we will become a small package and our lives will be shallow and empty. If we spend too much time on our tangible or physical possessions, we will neglect our spiritual or intangible side. We need a balance to keep us happy.

1. Read D&C 46:8-9: *"Seek ye earnestly the best gifts ... for they are given for the benefit of those who love me and keep all my commandments."* Also Timothy 4:14: *"Neglect not the gift that is within thee."*

2. Read the *Spiritual Gifts* envelope to find lasting gifts.

3. On the *Spiritual Gifts* envelope, list ways that you can focus on spiritual gifts (for example, read scriptures, Church books, and magazines; attend Church meetings; listen to LDS motivational tapes and music; turn off the TV, pray to get well when sick, get help with needs, or for spiritual gifts).

4. Play a matching game with the gift cards. If using several sets of cards, have young women place their initials on back of cards to retrieve later.

CREATE A SPIRITUAL GIFTS BOX:

Wrap a beautiful box that opens for each young women, one that she can cherish, to remember her spiritual gifts. Ask the young women to take small slips of paper and write on them special talents, gifts, and positive character traits they see in each young woman. If there are ten young women, they should all receive ten notes for their box, plus notes from leaders. Ask young women not to talk during this time so girls can feel inspired as they write.

EXCHANGE SPIRITUAL GIFTS:

Assign Gifts: The week before this activity, have each young woman draw another young woman's name. They should then thoughtfully select an item they have at home that they can give to the young woman to remind her of her gifts. For example, a magnet could represent a "magnetic" personality; a plum could say she is "plum" nice; a jug of water (she has a pure heart and mind); a bolt (she's like a "bolt of lightning", fun to be around); a diaper pin (she's good with children), a picture of Jesus (she follows in His steps). Girls might even draw a picture, write a poem, or find some poetry that describes this person.

Wrap and Present Gifts: Ask young women to wrap gifts in white paper and present the individual gifts in the group. Explain that the white paper represents the white fruit known as the gospel that Lehi beheld in the tree of life (1 Nephi 8:10-35). White is also the value color for faith. If we have faith in Jesus Christ, we can obtain spiritual gifts.

Price: ?

Please come to a Personal Progress activity!

Date:
Time:
Place:
Bring:

Have You Set a Price On Your Individual Worth?

You've Made Your Individual Worth Priceless

Certificate of Achievement
Awarded to

_____

for achieving your Individual Worth
Personal Progress goals!

_____   _____
Young Women Leader   Date

Priceless

Realize You Are a Daughter of Heavenly Father Who Loves You

Individual Worth – Value Experience #1:

SEARCH AND PONDER:

Psalm 8:4-6, Jeremiah 1:5, John 13:34

Doctrine and Covenants 18:10, and Abraham 3:22-23

How These Scriptures Teach Me That Heavenly Father Loves Me and Is Mindful of Me:

Scripture: Teachings:

_____

_____

_____

_____

_____

_____

_____

_____

_____

_____

_____

_____

Learn to Plan and Prepare

Individual Worth — Value Experience #2:

SEARCH AND PONDER:

Doctrine and Covenants 88:119

My List of My Hopes and Dreams for My Future:

My Home: _____

_____

My Family: _____

_____

_____

My Education: _____

_____

Things I Want to Accomplish In My Life:	Plan to Achieve These Goals:
_____	_____
_____	_____
_____	_____
_____	_____
_____	_____
_____	_____

Build Other's Self-worth

Individual Worth — Value Experience #3:

SEARCH AND PONDER:

Doctrine and Covenants 18:10 and 121:45

For Two Weeks I Notice the Following in Others
And Acknowledged These Qualities to Them in Writing:

Person(s):   Worthwhile Qualities and Attributes:

_____

_____

_____

_____

_____

_____

Week #1: M __ T __ W __ T __ F __ S __ S __
Week #2: M __ T __ W __ T __ F __ S __ S __

What I Have Learned about the Worth of Individuals and
How My Own Confidence Grows When I Build Others:

_____

_____

_____

_____

Participate in a Performance

Individual Worth – Value Experience #4:

I Participated in a Dance, Speech, Music, or Drama Performance at School ___, at Church ___, or in the Community ___.

The Type of Performance: _____

_____

_____

How this Activity Strengthened My Feelings of Individual Worth and Self-confidence:

_____

_____

_____

_____

_____

_____

_____

If possible keep a program from this event in my notebook.

Learn about Your Family History

Individual Worth — Value Experience #5:

I visited my living relative(s) to learn as much
information as possible about my family history.

Relative(s) I visited: _____

_____

_____

_____

I completed a pedigree chart of my family and listed the temple
ordinances that have been completed for each person.

Summary of My Discoveries:

_____

_____

_____

_____

_____

_____

_____

_____

Include the pedigree chart and my notes from this visit in my notebook.

Learn about Patriarchal Blessings

Individual Worth – Value Experience #6:

I Learned about the Importance of Patriarchal Blessings:

Why They Are Given: _____

_____

_____

Who Can Give Them: _____

How to Prepare for One: _____

_____

_____

_____

I Discussed this with My Parent or Leader. How a
Patriarchal Blessing Can Guide My Life: _____

_____

_____

_____

_____

I Am Preparing to Receive My Patriarchal Blessing By: _____

_____

_____

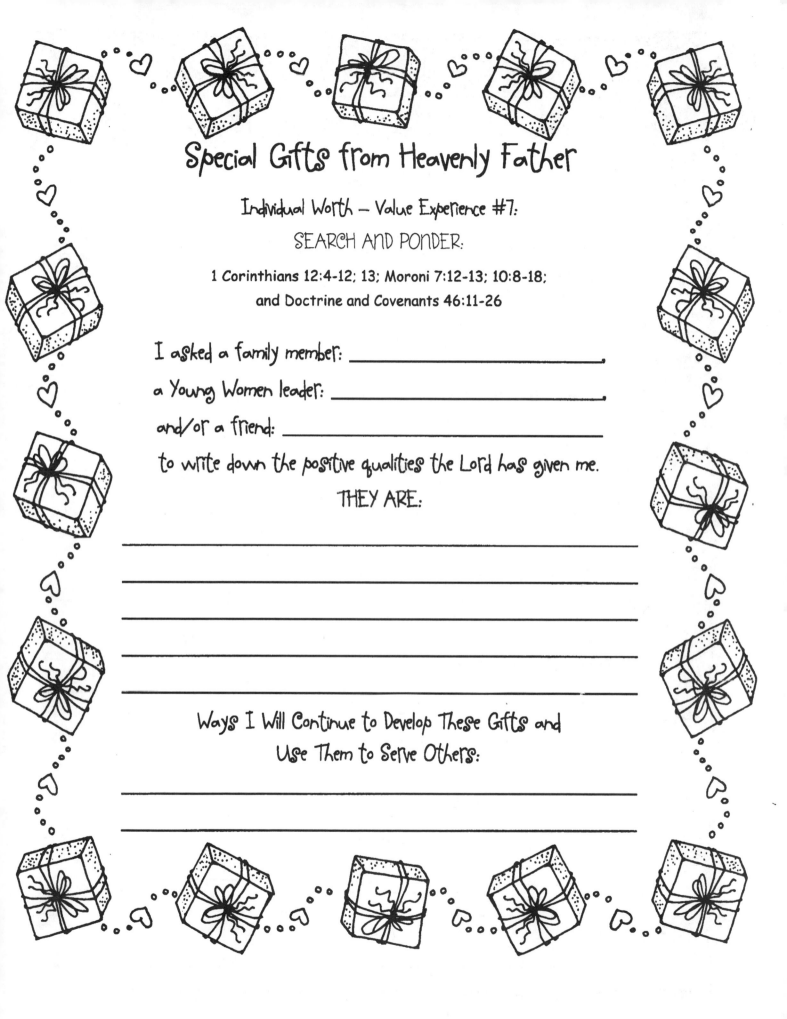

Special Gifts from Heavenly Father

Individual Worth — Value Experience #7:

SEARCH AND PONDER:

1 Corinthians 12:4-12; 13; Moroni 7:12-13; 10:8-18;
and Doctrine and Covenants 46:11-26

I asked a family member: _____

a Young Women leader: _____

and/or a friend: _____

to write down the positive qualities the Lord has given me.

THEY ARE:

_____

_____

_____

_____

Ways I Will Continue to Develop These Gifts and
Use Them to Serve Others:

_____

_____

Individual Worth Value Project Planner

My Project Is:

_____

_____

_____

_____

Steps to Carry Out My Project:

1. _____
2. _____
3. _____
4. _____
5. _____
6. _____
7. _____
8. _____

How I Felt about the Project:

_____

_____

_____

How My Understanding of Individual Worth Increased with this Project:

_____

_____

_____

Midweek Motivational Activities:

Value: Knowledge
Theme: We Seek Opportunities for Learning and Growth

Invitation and Certificates: (1) *Copy the invitation and
certificate (page 58) for each young woman. (2) *Color and cut out
images and fill in details. (3) To make invitation, cut on the top
dotted line, glue where shown, and fold book cover page to open book.
Deliver a week ahead. (4) See #5 below to distribute certificate.

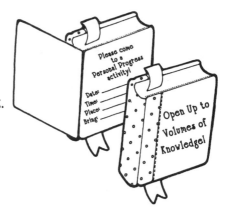

Goal Planning and Sharing: You'll need a *copy of the
Knowledge Value Experience #1-7 planners and the Knowledge Value
Project Planner (pages 51-58) for each young woman.

DISTRIBUTE FORMS AND HAVE ONE OR MORE ACTIVITIES
FROM THE FOLLOWING PAGES "FUN WAYS TO TEACH
VALUES":

1. Tell young women, that it is to our
benefit to continually seek opportunities
for learning and growth. Read Doctrine and
Covenants 88:118 (shown on page 33 in the
Personal Progress booklet).
2. Give each young woman a set of
Knowledge Value Experience #1-7 planners
and a Value Project Planner (sample shown
left). Review each planner #1-7 titles, e.g.,
#1: "Learn about the Importance of Gaining
Knowledge."
3. Suggest that they use the planners as
worksheets to plan and carry out their
goals and as a journal to record their experiences. When young women have passed off their goals,
they can record these in their Personal Progress journal, if desired.
4. Suggest that they post the planners on the mirror as a reminder.
When complete, store them in a looseleaf notebook or
folder (see Introduction).
5. Award a Knowldege certificate and a quilt block to young
women who have achieved all their Knowledge goals. See
the Appendix to make the quilt.

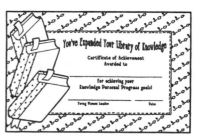

*All images shown in this book can be printed in color or black and white from the
Young Women Fun-tastic! Personal Progress Motivators CD-ROM.

Fun Ways to Teach Values:

Choose one or more of the following activities to motivate goal achievement.

KNOWLEDGE — VALUE EXPERIENCE #1: GAINING KNOWLEDGE

"CHEW"SING A CAREER! GUM WRAPPED PROS AND CONS:
To Make: Print the pattern (shown left) from the *Personal Progress* CD-ROM*. Or, copy or print the pattern from the *Young Women Fun-tastic! Activities – Manual 1* book or CD-ROM (Lesson #46). *Color, cut out (cutting slits in poster), wrap a stick of gum in each wrapper, and insert into slits.
Activity: Give the *"Chew"sing a Career* poster with gum wrapped in the *Career Pro and Con* wrappers to young women, and discuss possible home careers and the advantages of doing work in the home as they raise their family. Write pros and cons on wrappers and slide into a slot indicating career choices.

"PIG" (PRETTY INTELLIGENT GIRL) SEMINAR:
Have a PIG brainstorm before the seminar where young women and leaders can share their "Pretty Intelligent Girl" study habits.
1. Tell young women that pigs are very intelligent animals and can teach us a lot. PIGs can also mean "Pretty Intelligent Girls," so invite young women to "hoof on over" with a notebook and pen to learn about professions.
2. Invite four or five of the best professionals you can find to teach a 15-minute seminar on their profession. Have them talk about the ups and downs and pros and cons of their profession.
3. Tell young women that the more they learn about various professions, the better chance they will have of getting there. If they wait until their college years to know what they want, they may waste precious time and money.

I GIVE A HOOT! ABOUT MY VOCATION FUTURE FOCUS PLANNER:
To Make: Print the pattern (shown left) from the *Personal Progress* CD-ROM*. Or, copy or print the pattern from the *Young Women Fun-tastic! Activities – Manual 3* book or CD-ROM (Lesson #45). *Color.
Activity: Give the *I Give a Hoot!* planner to each young woman and talk about the owl, who symbolizes being wise, patient, and introspective (can see in the dark). Read D&C 9:7-9 and say, "If we pray about our choices, we can see through obscurity [clouded darkness] as the wise owl is able to do." Have young women focus on their future by completing this planner form for each vocational choice. Give young women several forms to plan each career they are thinking about. Encourage them to pray about their future vocation(s). Encourage young women to consider at least one home career (vocation) to earn money while they raise their children.

*All images shown in this book can be printed in color or black and white from the
Young Women Fun-tastic! Personal Progress Motivators CD-ROM.

60

NOBLE CAREER:

Pull scriptures and quotes from prophets and General Authorities that talk about careers and vocations and the role of women. Impress upon them a desire to first fulfill their responsibilities as wives and mothers, the most noble career. Assure them that knowledge and skills are very important. Guide them through choices that can give them great satisfaction and joy in both areas (work and family). Talk about reserving full-time careers for the right time and the importance of family first. Speakers could give tours of their home businesses, or explain how their career choices allow their family to come first.

STEPS TO CHOOSE CAREERS:

Encourage young women to take the time to choose one or more careers so they can begin planning for their future.

Tell Young Women: "We should get as much learning as possible, because we never know what might happen, or if we will have the opportunity to get married. Of course, the home is the highest calling when we are at that point; but it doesn't always necessarily work out that way. We need work skills before we're married, while we are married, and after the kids are grown."

Ideas: ❀ Learn about career choices. ❀ Learn about educational opportunities in your area. ❀ Learn about scholarships. ❀ Discuss subjects that will help with vocation and family life. ❀ Learn good personal study habits. ❀ Review school grades to determine how you can improve and increase study time and efficiency.

STUDY HABITS:

Share good study habits. Ralph Waldo Emerson said, "Concentration is the secret of strength."
Ideas: ❀ Organize. ❀ Schedule time. ❀ Study in the same place every day. ❀ Study without television, distracting music, and friends. ❀ Pray and ask for the Spirit to be with you. ❀ Write vocabulary and spelling words and items to memorize on cards and post on the mirror. ❀ Take short breaks, and then get right back to studying.

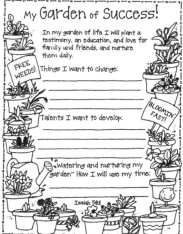

KNOWLEDGE — VALUE EXPERIENCE #2:
TALENTS TO CHERISH AND DEVELOP

MY SUCCESS GARDEN GOAL PLANNER:

To Make: Print the pattern (shown right) from the *Personal Progress CD-ROM**. Or, copy or print the pattern from the *Young Women Fun-tastic! Activities – Manual 1* book or CD-ROM (Lesson #41). *Color.
Activity: Using the *My Garden of Success!* planner, encourage young women to plant in their garden of life things that are of great worth and value (testimony, education, love for family and friends). Remind them they must—(1) *Weed Their Garden:* Read 2 Nephi 8:3 and write things they want to change. (2) *Plant Their Garden:* Read D&C 59:17-18 and write talents they want to develop. (3) *Water and Nurture Their Garden:* Read Isaiah 58:11 and decide how they will use their time and energy to create a successful garden.

HIDDEN TALENT NIGHT:

1. Research each young woman and have several people she knows tell you of a talent she has. Spotlight each young woman by reading a paragraph about her.

2. Gather pictures of each young woman and display them along with a typewritten spotlight.

3. Put a number under each photo displayed on a table. Have young women go around and write something about each young woman on a sheet of cardstock paper in front of picture. You may want to do this before the spotlight.

4. Gather the comments and place them in an envelope with her picture so young women can take these home. They can read and reread the comments and perhaps learn about talents they didn't know they had.

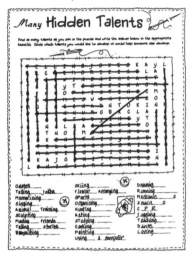

HIDDEN TALENTS CROSSWORD PUZZLE:

To Make: Print the pattern (shown left) from the *Personal Progress* CD-ROM*. Or, copy or print the pattern from the *Young Women Fun-tastic! Activities – Manual 1* book or CD-ROM (Lesson #47). *Color.

Activity: Using the *Many Hidden Talents* puzzle, help young women find the many talents they can develop throughout their life then highlight talents they wish to pursue.

HAVE A CASUAL TALENT NIGHT:

Have young women share their talents, e.g., piano, flute, guitar, craft skill, cooking demos, singing, scrapbooks, crafts. Display items they made and have them tell about their hobbies and interests and how they got started. Find an interest or talent from each girl to spotlight.

TALENTS, SKITS, AND BANANA SPLITS:

Have an evening with young men and women to share their talents or put on skits. End the evening with banana splits. Have young men and women tell you ahead of time their talent and how many minutes they will need to perform, then make up the program.

MY BASKET FULL OF TALENTS TALENTED EGG SHOW:

To Make: Print the pattern (shown right) from the *Personal Progress* CD-ROM*. Or, copy or print the pattern from the *Young Women Fun-tastic! Activities – Manual 2* book or CD-ROM (Less. #44). *Color and cut out basket, cutting a slit in basket. Fold the egg cards and glue back-to-back. Place egg cards in the slit.

ACTIVITY: Using the *Talent Basket,* show young women that their life is like a basket the can fill with talents and that we must work to develop them. This work can bring great joy. Heavenly Father has given us the potential to develop nearly any talent we wish. We can choose what we put in our basket of talents. So let's be a "good egg" and develop our talents.

*All images shown in this book can be printed in color or black and white from the
Young Women Fun-tastic! Personal Progress Motivators CD-ROM.

62

PARABLE OF THE TALENTS TALENT NIGHT:

Have a talent night and invite the parents.

Ideas: (1) Review the Parable of the Talents. Use coins for theme decorations and give refreshments with a gold coin (chocolate candy wrapped in gold paper) for the favor. (2) Play oldies songs and have girls do a lip sync with it. You could assign two songs to each class and invite the parents, and even the bishopric and Young Women leaders to join you. (3) Do a few musical numbers. (4) Model clothing someone has made. (5) Display artwork. (6) Do a variety of readings. (7) Give young women a pretty piece of paper and a pencil to write down talents they wish to develop. (8) Talk about various talents, and have a speaker or two tell briefly how they developed their talent. (9) Tell of the 1% inspiration and 99% perspiration theory—that talents take time and effort. (10) Take young women on a "talent trek" across the room. Mark a talent trail with crepe paper taped to the floor to mark the path to talents displayed.

TALENT TASTING TABLE:

Have young women volunteer to bring casseroles, salads, or desserts they make themselves. Ask someone to gather and type up the recipes and have them ready.

KNOWLEDGE — VALUE EXPERIENCE #4: UNDERSTAND A GOSPEL PRINCIPLE

❧ *Gospel Principles: Fasting, Sabbath Day,*
See Faith — Value Experience #3
❧ *Gospel Principle: Repentance*
See Choice and Accountability — Value Experience #4
❧ *Gospel Principle: Chastity*
See Choice and Accountability — Value Experience #6
❧ *Gospel Principle: Agency*
See Choice and Accountability — Value Experience #3

❧ *Gospel Principle: Eternal Life*

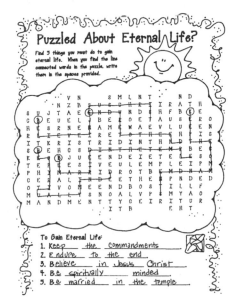

PUZZLED ABOUT ETERNAL LIFE:

To Make: Print the pattern (shown right) from the *Personal Progress* CD-ROM*. Or, copy or print the pattern from the *Young Women Fun-tastic! Activities – Manual 3* book or CD-ROM (Lesson #15). *Color the puzzle.

Activity: Using the *Puzzled About Eternal Life?* puzzle, help young women review the five ways we can *obtain the celestial kingdom with this fun connected word find.* Answers: keep the commandments, endure to the end, believe in Jesus Christ, be spiritually minded, and be married in the temple.

HOUSE OF ISRAEL DISCUSSION:
Have a patriarch come and explain the House of Israel and the blessings associated with it, using maps, etc.

NEPHI'S EMOTIONAL PLEA:
Read and discuss carefully 2 Nephi 3.

ETERNAL LIFE NIGHT:
Divide young women into five groups. Ask each group to design a booth to represent one of the five ways we can gain eternal life (noted above): (1) Keep the commandments. (2) Endure to the end. (3) Believe in Jesus Christ. (4) Be spiritually minded. (5) Be married in the temple.
Give young women some time on Sunday during class to discuss the design of their booth. That night, as a group, ask each booth committee to present their ideas. *Ideas:* Copy articles from the Church magazines. Create favors to give away, post pictures (found in the ward library). Have speaker or young woman give a 2 ½ minute talk on the above.

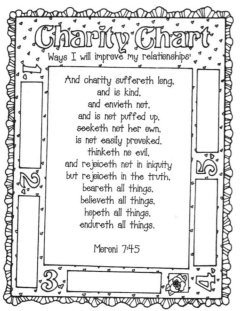

❊ *Gospel Principle: Charity*

CHARITY CHART CHALLENGE:
To Make: Print the pattern (shown left) from the *Personal Progress* CD-ROM*. Or, copy or print the pattern from the *Young Women Fun-tastic! Activities – Manual 3* book or CD-ROM (Lesson #43). *Color the chart.
Activity: Give each young woman a *Charity Chart* to memorize Moroni 7:45 and think of five ways they can improve their relationship with at least one person. Write these five ways on the border of the *Charity Chart*.

FRIENDSHIP:
Encourage young women to give their best ideas on how to acquire friends and be a friend. Tell them that these skills will help them in relationships with their family, friends, dates, and eventually a marriage friendship.
A friend is someone with whom you have common interests, share basic values, and learn to accept.
Ideas: ❊Look people in the eye when you speak to them. ❊ Show gratitude. ❊ Confide in someone. ❊Apologize and admit when you are wrong. ❊ Be forgiving. ❊Simply listen rather than give advice. ❊ Be interested. ❊ Thank others for help or compliments they give you. ❊ Help that friend feel important; someone said "It's nice to feel like you're that person's only friend; even though you know you are not." ❊ Be attentive—if others say "hello," or want to enter into the conversation, include them without excluding the friend you are talking to. ❊ Remember names. ❊ Be careful not to stretch your energy too far (you need time for yourself and your family). ❊ Find a common subject of interest about which you can communicate. ❊ Let others know you want their friendship instead of assuming they will discover it on their own.

*All images shown in this book can be printed in color or black and white from the
Young Women Fun-tastic! Personal Progress Motivators CD-ROM.

64

FRIENDSHIPS WITH YOUNG MEN:

Remind young women to treat young men as friends by paying attention to their thoughts, feelings, and accomplishments. Hopefully you will marry a young man who is your best friend. "Happy is the man that getteth understanding" (Proverbs 3:13). Communicate from the start. Share your likes and dislikes, and believe in his potential to serve a mission and to serve the Lord.

"PICK"-ET A FRIEND:

Gather young women and make picket signs, e.g., "We love Rachel," etc. Go to the young woman's home, and picket her home. Stick little signs on her lawn expressing love and friendship, e.g. "You are tops!," "We love you," or "You're super!" Leave a plate of cookies on the porch with an invitation to young women. This could also be done with several young women or young men. If they are at home, sit on the porch and chat while you and your friend eat the cookies.

KNOWLEDGE — VALUE EXPERIENCE
#5: LEARN ABOUT AN AREA OF WORK AND SERVICE
Also see Divine Nature — Value Experience #3.

ATTITUDE DETERMINES SUCCESS ATTITUDE ADJUSTER JOURNAL:

To Make: Print the pattern (shown right) from the *Personal Progress* CD-ROM*. Or, copy or print the pattern from the *Young Women Fun-tastic! Activities - Manual 1* book or CD-ROM (Lesson #45). *Color.

Activity: Use this *My Attitude Determines My Success* attitude adjuster journal to help young women evaluate what their attitude might be in challenging situations.

1. Write down the results of a negative and a positive attitude in a challenging situation.

2. Talk about work situations and how we struggle to complete tasks. Work can be a drudgery or a joy, depending upon our attitude. For example, a family took care of an elderly grandparent, helping her through each day to overcome the handicaps of old age. They said that when they were negative, it caused stress to the grandparent and stress to the family. When they were positive and patient, it brought the family joy and peace.

My Attitude Determines My Success

Challenge:	Result of a Negative Attitude:	Result of a Positive Attitude:
School Classes		
Baby-sitting		
Developing Talents		
Church Calling		
Home Tasks		
Part-time Job		

Work can be a rewarding experience or drudgery depending on your attitude! With each challenge, write about the results of a negative attitude and a positive attitude. Think about your own situation and what you would change to make it more positive.

FIND SOME FARM WORK:

Find a farm and see if young women can do some work on the farm, e.g., feed the birds and animals, milk cows, stack hay, rake, clean, etc.

UNUSUAL TASKS:

Find unique things for young women to do that will benefit the community or them personally. Have all young women help on specific projects, e.g., wash cars, organize with ward members to cater a ward banquet, supply entertainment for ward functions, do dishes after ward activities, put on a play involving children, work with the mentally and physically handicapped, find and adopt a grandparent, entertain at a convalescent center, visit those in nursing homes or rehabilitation centers, organize a patriotic parade, design and put on a play that teaches children or young women values, invite parents to participate in service projects, go on a good will drive to collect items for the needy, cook for a homeless shelter and serve them.

KNOWLEDGE — VALUE EXPERIENCE #6: ATTEND AND EVALUATE A PERFORMANCE
See Individual Worth — Value Experience #4

MUSEUM SHOW-AND-TELL:

At a museum divide young women into groups to scope out the museum in sections. Then get together and have young women show and tell about what they have learned being the tour guides for their portion of the museum. Take photos to place on the I Love Cultural Arts! frame/journal (previewed on page 45) and write about your findings and experience.

KNOWLEDGE — VALUE EXPERIENCE #7:
DEVELOP THE SKILLS OF STORYTELLING

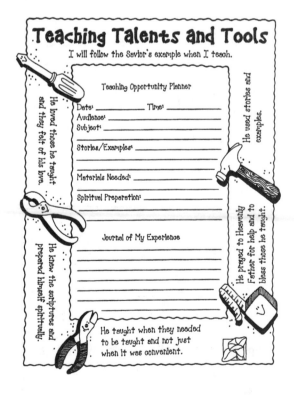

TEACHING TALENTS AND TOOLS JOURNAL:

To Make: Print the pattern (shown left) from the *Personal Progress* CD-ROM*. Or, copy or print the pattern from the *Young Women Fun-tastic! Activities - Manual 3* book or CD-ROM (Lesson #6). *Color.

Activity: Help young women learn to follow the Savior's example when they teach. Use this *Teaching Talents and Tools* journal to help them plan their next teaching assignment. Coordinate an opportunity for the young women to teach Primary (e.g., while Relief Society and priesthood meet together in a joint meeting). Talk about the tools that Jesus used when he taught (found in the border). Help young women plan, carry out, and have a positive teaching experience. If teaching opportunities are not available, young women could use this to prepare and carry out a family home evening presentation.

*All images shown in this book can be printed in color or black and white from the
Young Women Fun-tastic! Personal Progress Motivators CD-ROM.

66

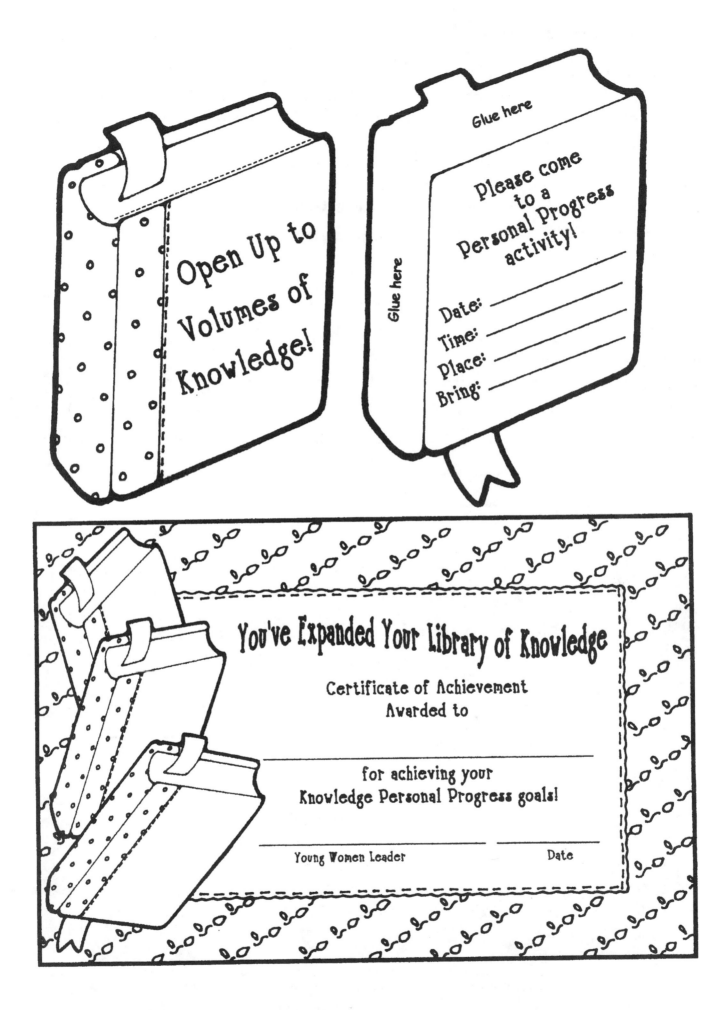

Open Up to Volumes of Knowledge!

Glue here

Glue here

Please come to a Personal Progress activity!

Date: _____
Time: _____
Place: _____
Bring: _____

You've Expanded Your Library of Knowledge

Certificate of Achievement
Awarded to

_____

for achieving your
Knowledge Personal Progress goals!

_____   _____
Young Women Leader   Date

Learn about the Importance of Gaining Knowledge

Knowledge – Value Experience #1:

SEARCH AND PONDER:

Proverbs 1:5; 4:7; 2 Nephi 28:30; and

Doctrine and Covenants 88:78-80, 118; 90:15; 130:18-19; 131:6

What I Have Learned About Knowledge from these Scriptures:

_____

_____

_____

_____

_____

_____

_____

How Knowledge and Understanding of Gospel Principles Applies in the Present and in the Future to Me, My Family, and My Home:

_____

_____

_____

_____

_____

_____

_____

_____

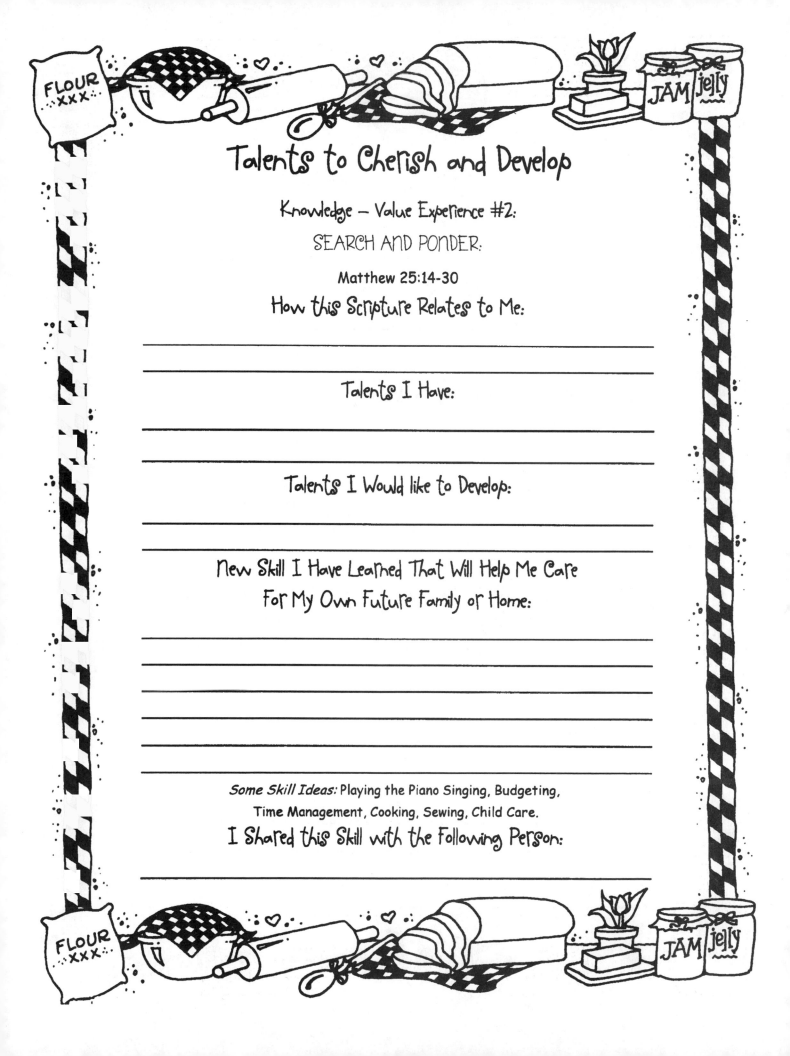

Talents to Cherish and Develop

Knowledge – Value Experience #2:

SEARCH AND PONDER:

Matthew 25:14-30

How this Scripture Relates to Me:

_____

_____

Talents I Have:

_____

_____

Talents I Would like to Develop:

_____

_____

New Skill I Have Learned That Will Help Me Care
For My Own Future Family or Home:

_____

_____

_____

_____

_____

Some Skill Ideas: Playing the Piano Singing, Budgeting,
Time Management, Cooking, Sewing, Child Care.

I Shared this Skill with the Following Person:

_____

Appreciate Hymns

Knowledge – Value Experience #3:

I Memorized the Following Two Hymns:

Hymn #1: _____ Number _____

Hymn #2: _____ Number _____

I Learned the Following Conducting Patterns for the Hymns:

_____

_____

_____

_____ I Conducted These Hymns in Family Home Evening,

Young Women, Another Church Meeting, or Seminary.

From the Hymns Listed Above, I Read the
Following Scriptures Listed at the End of Each Hymn:

Hymn #:   Scripture: My Thoughts:

_____

_____

_____

_____

_____

_____

_____

_____

_____

_____

Understand a Gospel Principle

Knowledge — Value Experience #4:

I Selected One a Gospel Principles I Would like to Understand Better:

_____

I Read the Following Scriptures and Talks That Relate
To My Chosen Gospel Principle (Above):

_____

_____

_____

_____

I Gave a Five-minute Talk on the Subject in Sacrament Meeting, a
Young Women Meeting, to My Family, or Young Women Class.
Outline of the Talk:

_____

_____

_____

_____

_____

_____

_____

_____

Learn about an Area Of Work or Service

Knowledge — Value Experience #5:

The Field of Work That Interests Me:

_____

Someone Who Works in this Field of Interest:

Name: _____ Phone: _____

Their Work Responsibilities:

_____

_____

_____

_____

Training or Education They Have Obtained to Do Their Job:

_____

_____

What Contributions this Person's Job Makes in Society:

_____

Attend and Evaluate a Performance

Knowledge – Value Experience #6:

Memorize the Thirteenth Article of Faith and Recite It:

"We believe in being honest, true, chaste, benevolent, virtuous, and in doing good to all men; indeed, we may say that we follow the admonition of Paul—We believe all things, we hope all things we have endured many things, and hope to be able to endure all things. If there is anything virtuous, lovely, or of good report or praiseworthy, we seek after these things."

I Visited a Museum or Exhibit or Attended a Performance That Involves Dance, Music, Speech, or Drama as Follows:

_____

Using the 13th Article of Faith as a Guide, I Saw and Heard the Following as I Visited the Museum or Exhibit or Attended the Performance:

_____

_____

_____

_____

_____

_____

_____

_____

Develop the Skills of Storytelling

Knowledge – Value Experience #7:

Someone Whose Stories I Have Enjoyed Hearing:

_____

I Discussed with this Person Their Storytelling Skills:

_____

_____

I Learned How to Select Stories for Specific Audiences:

_____

_____

_____

I Learned How to Enhance the Story With:

My Voice: _____

_____

My Facial Expressions: _____

_____

My Gestures: _____

_____

I Shared the Following Stories with My Family,
Young Women or Primary Classes, or Other Audiences.

Story #1: _____

Story #2: _____

Knowledge Value Project Planner

My Project Is:

_____

_____

_____

_____

Steps to Carry Out My Project:

1. _____
2. _____
3. _____
4. _____
5. _____
6. _____
7. _____
8. _____

How I Felt about the Project:

_____

_____

How My Understanding of Knowledge Increased with this Project:

_____

_____

_____

Midweek Motivational Activities:
Value: Choice and Accountability
Theme: We Choose the Good, Accepting Responsibility for Decisions

Invitation and Certificates: (1) *Copy the invitation and certificate (pages 94-95) for each young woman. (2) *Color and cut out images and fill in details. (3) To make invitation, glue parts A to part B and fan-fold to close. Deliver a week ahead. (4) See #5 below to distribute certificate.

Goal Planning and Sharing: You'll need a *copy of the Choice and Accountability Value Experience #1-7 planners and the Choice and Accountability Value Project Planner (pages 96-103) for each young woman.

DISTRIBUTE FORMS AND HAVE ONE OR MORE ACTIVITIES FROM THE FOLLOWING PAGES "FUN WAYS TO TEACH VALUES":

1. Tell young women that we are free to choose good over evil and accept responsibility for our decisions. Read Joshua 24:15 (shown on page 40 in the Personal Progress booklet).

2. Give each young woman a set of Choice and Accountability Value Experience #1-7 planners and a Value Project Planner (sample shown left). Review each planner #1-7 titles, e.g., #1: "*A Daughter of God Can Make Wise Decisions and Solve Problems.*"

3. Suggest that they use the planners as worksheets to plan and carry out their goals and as a journal to record their experiences. When young women have passed off their goals, they can record these in their Personal Progress journal.

4. Suggest that they post the planners on the mirror as a reminder. When complete, store them in a looseleaf notebook or folder (see Introduction).

5. Award a Choice and Accountability certificate and a quilt block to young women who have achieved all their Choice and Accountability goals. See the Appendix to make the quilt.

*All images shown in this book can be printed in color or black and white from the *Young Women Fun-tastic! Personal Progress Motivators* CD-ROM.

Fun Ways to Teach Values:
Choose one or more of the following activities to motivate goal achievement.

CHOICE AND ACCOUNTABILITY
— VALUE EXPERIENCE #1:
MAKE WISE DECISIONS AND SOLVE PROBLEMS

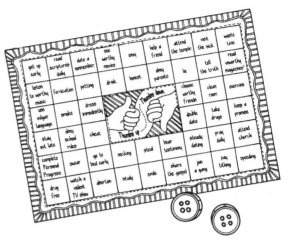

THUMBS UP OR DOWN CHOICES GAME:

To Make: Print the pattern (shown right) from the *Personal Progress CD-ROM**. Or, copy or print the pattern from the *Young Women Fun-tastic! Activities – Manual 2* book or CD-ROM (Lesson #35). *Color.

Activity: Use this game to help young women understand that the consequences of their actions are not always immediate but they can affect their lives. Young women can vote if the choices are right or wrong and tell consequences for making each choice.

FUTURE FOCUS:

Project young women into the future with the choices they could make, e.g., live your life with the end in mind. Read the part of Steven Covey's book *The Seven Habits of Effective People* (pp. 96-99) about going to your own funeral.

• Have them ponder these questions: Where will I be if . . . ?, how will I look if . . . ? and what will I be if . . . ? Ask the question: Do we marry the people we date?

Project into the Future with These Situations: (1) You choose to marry a nonmember. (2) You choose to marry an active member. (3) You choose to marry a less-active member. (4) What if I don't live the Word of Wisdom? (5) What will my life be like if I wear immodest clothing?

• Try to see the end result of choices. Tell them that when you pick up a stick the other end comes with it.

• Read Alma 48:11-18 (a description of a future companion). Keep in mind that young women should achieve these traits as well if they are to attract a future companion they admire.

• Have people who have experienced good and bad choices talk to them.

WAYS TO FOLLOW JESUS TENT CARD:

To Make: Print the pattern (shown right) from the *Personal Progress CD-ROM**. Or, copy or print the pattern from the *Young Women Fun-tastic! Activities – Manual 1* book or CD-ROM (Lesson #11). *Color, cut out, and fold card to stand up.

Activity: Using this tent card, help young women memorize D&C 29:1-2 and talk about the maturity that comes from listening and following the Savior. Have them write ways they will follow the Savior Jesus Christ (be humble, pray, listen to the Lord, obey the commandments, serve others, read the scriptures, attend church).

All images shown in this book can be printed in color or black and white from the Young Women Fun-tastic! Personal Progress Motivators CD-ROM.

"I THINK I CAN" CLASSES:
Set up several classes for the young women: one on budget by a CPA, one on job interviews by a person who hires, one on grooming by a beautician, one on organizing time by an organized individual, etc. Have a 15-minute class just to cover the basics. If there is a large group, you could break off into workshops and have the individual teach four times. If instructors are willing to give their name and phone number, write them on a special card to give to each girl. This way girls can call on them for advice.

CHOICE AND ACCOUNTABILITY — VALUE EXPERIENCE #2:
CHOOSE STANDARDS OF RIGHTEOUS BEHAVIOR

❀ *Standard: Honesty*
See Divine Nature — Value Experience #6

❀ *Standard: Media*

TV TOPPER AND BOOKSHELF BUDDY TENT CARDS:
To Make: Print the pattern (shown left) from the *Personal Progress* CD-ROM*. Or, copy or print the pattern from the *Young Women Fun-tastic! Activities – Manual 1* book or CD-ROM (Lesson #33). *Color, cut out, fold, and glue tabs so cards stand up.
Activity: Give each young woman a *TV Topper* and *Bookshelf Buddy* tent card to help them memorize quotes and decide what they can do to choose worthy television programs, movies, books, and magazines. Write the ideas on stand-up cards. Girls can place them on their television or bookshelf to remind them to be aware of media influences.

QUESTIONABLE MEDIA AND QUESTIONABLE COOKIES OR BROWNIES:
1. Prepare ahead chocolate chip cookies or brownies and have them ready on two separate plates (showing the same treat). Attach the following note to one of the plates of cookies or brownies:
Questionable Cookies
Questionable Brownies
2. With the two plates of cookies or brownies in front of girls, talk about movies, Hollywood standards, movie ratings, etc. Lead the discussion into phrases that people use after going to these movies. For example, "The movie isn't too bad," "There's only a little swearing," "Just a little talk about sex." "You didn't see much." "I've seen worse."
3. Tell young women you made some cookies or brownies with the best ingredients (real butter, highest grade chocolate chips). Then hold up the plate with the sign Questionable Cookies or Questionable Brownies and say, "What if I told you that in this batch I added a little bit of doggie-do? Just a little never hurt anyone. Try them. What would you do?"

4. After getting their reaction, say, "These are completely eatable cookies. There's really no doggie-do in them." Talk about ways Satan leads people "*carefully down to hell*," by adding just a little here and there (through desensitization).

5. Read 2 Nephi 28:21. While you enjoy the cookies or brownies, make some new resolves. Have young women always ask themselves before participating in media, "Do I like doggie-do in my brownies?"

TUG AT THE HEART STRINGS:

Have an evening of poetry reading at someone's house and feel your heart strings being tugged. Use soft lights and music to set a relaxed mood. Also read selected scriptures that show heartfelt emotion. Encourage young women to really think about this and come prepared with their favorite poetry, hymns, or scriptures to read.

CHOICE AND ACCOUNTABILITY — VALUE EXPERIENCE #3:
BLESSINGS AND RESPONSIBILITIES OF AGENCY

CONSEQUENCES QUIZ:

To Make: Print the pattern (shown right) from the *Personal Progress* CD-ROM*. Or, copy or print the pattern from the *Young Women Fun-tastic! Activities – Manual 2* book or CD-ROM (Lesson #28). *Color.

Activity:

1. *Read Scriptures:* Genesis 39 and tell about Joseph who was sold into Egypt when he resisted the advances of Potiphar's wife, how he ran (verse 12) from her because he had made up his mind ahead of time what to do. We can do the same by writing choices for the future in our own journal. Discuss the possible immediate, future, and eternal consequences if Joseph had not resisted temptation.

2. *Show Picture:* Obtain to show the picture "Joseph Resists Potipher's Wife," #62548 in your ward library. You will also find a picture of this in *The New Era*, July, 1999, with the caption that reads: "Joseph's personal integrity helped him make righteous choices even in difficult situations."

3. Give each young woman a *Consequence Quiz* to discuss how every choice has a consequence. Next to each choice, write the immediate consequence, the future consequence, and the eternal consequence of that choice or action.

4. *Panel Poll:* After completing the activity, divide young women into three groups, each representing a panel that comments on each decision. Panel #1 could have a strip of paper in front of them that reads "Immediate Consequences," Panel #2 has a "Future Life" sign, and Panel #3 has an "Eternal Consequences" sign. Read each choice and have the panel express their opinion about the choice.

All images shown in this book can be printed in color or black and white from the Young Women Fun-tastic! Personal Progress Motivators CD-ROM.

79

DEBTORS PRISON OR PARTNERS PARADISE:

Ahead of Time: Decorate the room with prison bars. Place a sign for "Debtors Prison" on one side and one for "Partners Paradise" on the other (add beautiful flowers and a pretty backdrop). Write good and bad choices on cards and tape cards on the walls face down. Prepare at least one or two cards for each young woman.

Activity: Read and discuss Mosiah 2:17-25.

1. Have young women stand in the center of the room as you explain that we owe Heavenly Father a great deal for the blessings we have. We can honor Him and uplift ourselves by living the commandments and making right choices. If we don't make right choices, we get deeper in debt. If we make right choices we grow more like Heavenly Father, and become a "partner in paradise." Point to the Partners Paradise corner. Paradise is a place where we are happy and loved.

2. Have young women take a card off the wall and take turns reading cards aloud to determine where they go, to Debtors Prison or Partners Paradise. Do this until everyone has had a turn and has gone to their destination.

3. Ask them how their own debts make them feel.

4. Ask them, "With the decision you read, how do you feel about where you are?" Give them a chance to respond. Ask, "Do you feel trapped?" "Do you feel free?"

5. Talk about repentance and service, bearing testimony, etc., as ways to pay back our debts.

APPLE PIE POSITIVE SELF-TALK SEMINAR:

Be prepared to show young women an apple and a fresh apple pie (hopefully one that is warm fresh out of the oven). Tell young women that it is easy to be just an apple, but with a little more effort we can be an apple pie. As we know, we are all children of God; we have the desire to be better. You may want to demonstrate how to make an apple pie. To become an apple pie we must add the sugar and butter to make caramel syrup. We add the spices and a rich tasty crust. Self-mastery is like that. You can accept yourself the way you are (show the apple) or we can add the things that make you even better than you are now (show the apple pie). Don't be afraid to tell yourself that you are of great worth and value. Add spice to your life by strengthening your character. List "Apple"ing Character Traits on the board.

Step #1: Have guest speakers come prepared to speak (see #3 below). Provide notepaper and pencils for young women with an apple and apple pie sticker.

Step #2: Ahead of time put up positive self-talk signs in the shapes of apples all over the room on the floor, ceiling, walls, table, light, and board. Ideas: "You're the apple of Heavenly Father's eye," "Bloom where you're planted," "Confidence is a gift you can give yourself," "Practice releases pressure," "If it is to be, it is up to me," "Nothing is too good to be true, nothing is too good to last," "Do your best and leave the rest," "Count to 10 and then start over again," "If at first you don't succeed . . . try, try again."

Step #3: Have a guest speaker tell how girls can make their life into an apple pie through building their character. *Ideas:* (1) Describe good self-talk and bad self-talk. Talk about what positive self-talk can do. (2) Search the scriptures to find the right and wrong way to care for yourself, e.g., the Word of Wisdom, commandments like fasting, exercising, etc.

Step #4: Have young women list five self-talk messages they wish to take home and memorize.

AGENCY ACTIONS SCRIPTURE CHALLENGE:

To Make: Print the pattern (shown right) from the *Personal Progress* CD-ROM*. Or, copy or print the pattern from the *Young Women Fun-tastic! Activities – Manual 3* book or CD-ROM (Lesson #24). *Color.

Activity: Give each young woman an *Agency Actions* scripture challenge to learn of those who followed Satan and those who followed Jesus Christ. Read D&C 58:28 to help young women know that they are agents unto themselves to choose evil or good. Tell them that "evil" spelled backwards is "live." As they "live" the gospel of Jesus Christ, they will gain freedom. Following Jesus Christ leads to liberty, eternal life, and joy. Observe people or the different countenances on the handout and talk about the peace and joy that radiates from righteous individuals, and the contrast between them and those who do not make right choices. If time allows, role-play some of the characters.

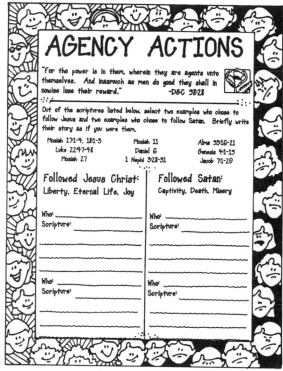

FREE AGENCY SCRIPTURE CHASE:

Have young women organize and compete in a scripture chase, dividing into two teams and racing to find situations in the scriptures that tell good and bad choices that were made. Tell how this choice affected others. If young women know the stories, ask them to tell them.

❀ Read scriptures to tell a story where someone followed Jesus Christ or chose to follow Satan.
❀ Read how Alma the Younger gave commandments and instruction to his sons Shiblon and Corianton (Alma 38-39). ❀ Talk about the importance of making decisions before the temptations come. This gives us more freedom to choose. We don't have to wait and think about the temptation; we already know what to say and what to do. ❀ (Genesis 37:36; 39) Tell of the example of Joseph in Egypt, who was tempted by Potiphar's wife. Tell how Joseph resisted the advances of Potiphar's wife. Talk about Joseph's reaction to her temptation, how he may have decided ahead of time what he would do if he was tempted in this way, because he immediately ran from the situation. If he had hesitated, he may have accepted her request and lost his eternal blessings. ❀ Talk about how we can make those critical choices in our lives.

*All images shown in this book can be printed in color or black and white from the
Young Women Fun-tastic! Personal Progress Motivators CD-ROM.

81

PICK A PATH TO ETERNAL LIFE DECISION MAKER MOBILE:

To Make: Print the pattern (shown left) from the *Personal Progress* CD-ROM*. Or, copy or print the pattern from the *Young Women Fun-tastic! Activities – Manual 1* book or CD-ROM (Lesson #17). *Color, cut out.

Activity: Give each young women a *Pick the Path to Eternal Life* mobile and help them pick the path by reading the scripture references below each stepping stone, writing in the stone the reward for following each path, and deciding which path you want to follow and color that path. Fold and glue mobile together, punch at the top in three places, and hang with a string.

PROMISES KEPT SCRIPTURE SITUATIONS SEARCH:

Search together in the scriptures for various situations when oaths were made and their circumstances. Why were these oaths made? What were they? Get a feeling for the importance of keeping covenants and promises (see *oaths, covenants, promise, swear, vow,* and *pledge* in the Index and Topical Guide).

"THE LORD NEVER BREAKS COVENANTS" OBJECT LESSON:

Have two people (a young woman and an adult priesthood holder or bishop) stand together with a metal or paper chain around them. Lock it (or pretend to lock it). Give the key to the young women. Say, "The adult represents the Lord and the young woman is you. You have the power to break a covenant or keep it binding. The Lord will never break a covenant. Only people do." Discuss how making and keeping covenants makes us strong and extraordinary.

CHOICE AND ACCOUNTABILITY — VALUE EXPERIENCE #4:

APPLY THE PRINCIPLES OF REPENTANCE IN YOUR LIFE

SUNSHINE REPENTANCE DOORKNOB SIGN:

To Make: Print the pattern (shown left) from the *Personal Progress* CD-ROM*. Or, copy or print the pattern from the *Young Women Fun-tastic! Activities – Manual 1* book or CD-ROM (Lesson #22). *Color, cut out, fold, and glue back-to-back.

Activity: Young women can create this doorknob hanger as a reminder that repentance helps us to move from darkness into the light. Write the steps to repentance found in the Young Women manual 1 as follows: (1) Recognize wrongdoing. (2) Promise never to repeat the sin. (3) Recommit to live the gospel. (4) Make restitution for wrongs: repent in prayer, confess to bishop, apologize to those offended. (5) Feel a depth of repentance as deep as the sin. (6) Prove ourselves worthy over time. (7) Forgive ourselves and those who have offended us. (8) Commit not to look back, but to accept the Lord's forgiveness.

*All images shown in this book can be printed in color or black and white from the *Young Women Fun-tastic! Personal Progress Motivators* CD-ROM.

82

MIGHTY CHANGE OF HEART:

Tell young women: "You can never really change until you change your heart! A changed heart is a repentant heart." Talk about the mighty change of heart discussed in the Book of Mormon. Have a special skit dramatizing a story in the Book of Mormon, e.g., Alma the Younger. Serve heart-shaped cupcakes or heart-shaped pancakes with strawberry syrup, strawberries and whipped cream. Make notes on hearts and then stick them on dozens of cars in the church parking lot on Sunday or in the mailbox of a special friend.

Repentance Fruit Roll-ups: Give each young woman a piece of fruit leather rolled up with a string attached, or inside a package. Tell them that before they "roll" into bed at night, think of things they may have done during the day that they need to repent of, and ask Heavenly Father for forgiveness. Then before they "roll" out of bed in the morning, pray that they can keep the commandments.

MY CHANGE OF HEART MOBILE:

To Make: Print the pattern (shown right) from the *Personal Progress* CD-ROM*. Or, copy or print the pattern from the *Young Women Fun-tastic! Activities – Manual 3* book or CD-ROM (Lesson #29).

Option: Copy mobile on two different colors of cardstock paper (so when the mobile turns, one side will be a different color from the other side). If you create this mobile in different colors it will be easier to see the right message as mobile turns.

To Assemble: Lay *My Change of Heart Steps #1-2* pieces ½-inch apart face down. Place a thin 1 ½ foot string down the center, taping the string to the #1-2 pieces on the blank side, leaving string at the top. Lay, and glue steps #3-4 pieces face-up over the matching steps #1-2 pieces. Make sure the long piece of the string is at the top to hang mobile.

Activity: Create a two-sided mobile to show young women the four steps King Benjamin's people went through to have a change of heart, reading Mosiah 5:2, 5. *Side One:* I will learn about Christ and his commandments.
I will have faith in Christ and believe in his Atonement. *Side Two:* I will ask for forgiveness, and be forgiven through the Lord's mercy. I will make a covenant to keep the commandments, and do good all my days.

CHANGE OF HEART ROLE-PLAY:

Have young women visit the ward library to find an article that expresses a change of heart. Have them rehearse and then act out the story in a five-minute play for the other young women.

*All images shown in this book can be printed in color or black and white from the
Young Women Fun-tastic! Personal Progress Motivators CD-ROM.

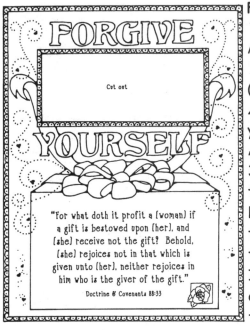

FORGIVE
Cut out
YOURSELF

"For what doth it profit a [woman] if
a gift is bestowed upon [her], and
[she] receive not the gift? Behold,
[she] rejoices not in that which is
given unto [her], neither rejoices in
him who is the giver of the gift."
Doctrine & Covenants 88:33

FORGIVE—MIRROR MESSAGE POSTER:

To Make: Print the pattern (shown left) from the *Personal Progress* CD-ROM*. Or, copy or print the pattern from the *Young Women Fun-tastic! Activities – Manual 3* book or CD-ROM (Lesson #27). *Color and cut out and cut out where indicated.

Activity: Tell young women self-love is a gift you can give yourself through repentance and the forgiving process. Read Alma the Younger's story of repentance and forgiveness (Alma 36:16-21). Present this *Forgive Yourself* mirror message poster to each young woman. Read D&C 88:33 as printed on the poster. Have young women take this home to hold up to their face as they look into the mirror, forgiving themselves of wrong choices they have made and telling themselves how they will change. Imagine this box as a television set within our minds. If we let our sins run over and over again in our minds, we are not letting the sins go. After we repent of a sin, we should never have reruns!

LETTING GO:

There is a principle of "letting go" that is taught when sailing a boat. If you hold on to the rope too tight you can tip the boat over. There needs to be a certain amount of control in holding on to the rope, but when it's time to let go and let the wind take over, you need to let go for smooth sailing. We too need to let go of our sins by repenting and forgiving ourselves. If we really realize that Jesus Christ suffered for us so that we can repent and be forgiven, we will let go of our guilt and make a fresh start. True repentance is acknowledging the Atonement; as with holding the rope too tightly, if we do not let Christ take our sins, then we will tip or even sink under the powerful winds of depression and guilt. With His Atonement we can be forgiven and we can sail back to our heavenly home. The seas of life are often rough as the waves of temptation, sin, and guilt rush over us; but we can endure if we start by forgiving ourselves.

1. Write on a piece of paper something you did that was wrong or unkind, etc. Do not include your name.
2. Fold the paper and place it on a helium balloon or around a stick or in a pinecone.
3. Then have a ceremony and talk about forgiveness and the healing power it has. Have an older girl (Laurel) give a talk about "Letting go of negative and unkind actions."
4. Have a silent prayer where girls can ask for forgiveness if they haven't already, and ask Heavenly Father to help you release these feelings.
5. Then let go of the balloons all at once, or go to a river and watch the sticks float away, or stand around a campfire and throw in your pine cones.
6. Resolve to never do that again. Take a deep breath, forgive yourself, and let it go!

*All images shown in this book can be printed in color or black and white from the *Young Women Fun-tastic! Personal Progress Motivators* CD-ROM.

84

CHOICE AND ACCOUNTABILITY
— VALUE EXPERIENCE #5:
LEARN ABOUT THE HOLY GHOST

LIGHT OF THE HOLY GHOST MOBILE:

To Make: Print the pattern (shown right) from the *Personal Progress* CD-ROM*. Or, copy or print the pattern from the *Young Women Fun-tastic! Activities – Manual 1* book or CD-ROM (Lesson #4). *Color and cut out, glue back-to-back, punch a hole, and tie a string on the top to hang.

ACTIVITY: Give each young woman a light bulb mobile and look up the scriptures for clues to the missing words. Answers:

• *Light Bulb Side #1* (*Be Worthy to Receive the Holy Ghost*): What we must do to be worthy of the companionship of the Holy Ghost. (1) repent, (2) commandments, (3) pray, (4) faith, (5) world, (6) baptized.

• *Light Bulb Side #2* (*Blessings of the Holy Ghost*): different ways that the Holy Ghost can bless our lives. *Answers:* (1) teach, (2) things, (3) truth, (4) record, (5) comforter, (6) mind, heart.

STOP AND SMELL THE FLOWERS—COMPARE TO THE SPIRIT OF THE HOLY GHOST:

1. Create a room full of clutter with a bouquet of flowers in the center of the table. Have dirty dishes on the table. Scatter magazines, papers, and clothes all over the floor. Have a dust cloth, vacuum, and a pan of dish soap and a dish cloth to wash dishes available. Ask young women to enter the room, sit down, and write down their feelings.

2. Ask young women to go out, but have a few stay and help clean up the room. Leave the bouquet of flowers in the center of the table.

3. Ask young women to come back into the room and write down their impressions. Say, "The bouquet of flowers you see can be compared to the Holy Ghost in our lives. The first time you saw this room, you saw a room full of clutter. You may not have noticed the flowers. But when the room was free of clutter, you might have seen the flowers first. This is how it is with the Holy Ghost. When our minds are free of clutter, we are free to listen to and enjoy Heavenly Father's spirit."

4. Make a list of things that clutter our lives that might prevent us from listening to the Spirit (for example, not doing homework, not going to church, not reading the scriptures, not helping around the house, not going to seminary, etc.)

5. Blindfold one of the young women, saying, "Sometimes we blindfold ourselves with things that don't matter and neglect the things that do matter."

6. Talk about the floral symbols assigned to each value (e.g., rose represents Individual Worth). Have them ask themselves what their life would be like without one of these values. Each value invites the Spirit of the Holy Ghost.

*All images shown in this book can be printed in color or black and white from the
Young Women Fun-tastic! Personal Progress Motivators CD-ROM.

85

CHOICE AND ACCOUNTABILITY –
VALUE EXPERIENCE #6:
PREPARE TO ENTER THE TEMPLE

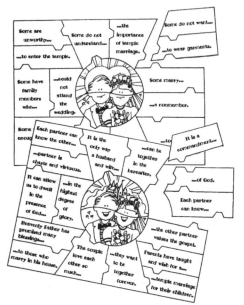

ETERNAL MARRIAGE PUZZLE QUIZ:

To Make: Print the patterns (shown left) from the *Personal Progress* CD-ROM*. Or, copy or print the patterns from the *Young Women Fun-tastic! Activities – Manual 1* book or CD-ROM (Lesson #18). *Color and cut out puzzles and place them all in one envelope for each young woman.

Activity: Have young women put both puzzles together at the same time, reading the clues that indicate which puzzle it belongs to. The puzzles represent (a) reasons young people give for wanting to marry in the temple, and (b) reasons some do not marry in the temple. Talk about the difference between the brides' and grooms' smiles and the feelings they may have for the choices they make to marry in the temple or outside the temple.

TEMPLE CHASE:

1. Get young women together and provide a pleasant setting with temple pictures around the room and/or displayed on tables.

2. Set out the scriptures as well as articles from Church magazines on the temple and eternal marriage. Have groups of young women find scriptures and read articles, etc., and report the various points they discover. Give each young woman a blank sheet of paper and a pen to write down the important points she finds.

3. Assign young women group leaders to share what they have learned.

4. Talk about inner strength and how we can resolve to always set our sights on the temple.

5. Discuss appropriate dress and talk about the questions in a recommend interview.

BAKE A TEMPLE CAKE:

Bake a sheet cake and frost. Cut into squares and place a temple or heart shaped mints or candy on top of each square. As young women enjoy the cake, ask them to think of the sweetness that comes to mind as they imagine themselves married for time and all eternity to the man they will someday come to love.

TEMPLE PREPARATION TENT CARD:

To Make: Print the pattern (shown left) from the *Personal Progress* CD-ROM*. Or, copy or print the pattern from the *Young Women Fun-tastic! Activities – Manual 2* book or CD-ROM (Lesson #15). *Color, cut out, and fold card to stand up.

*All images shown in this book can be printed in color or black and white from the *Young Women Fun-tastic! Personal Progress Motivators* CD-ROM.

Activity: Help young women create an eternal family by entering the right choices on their own personalized temple tent card. They can write things they will do to prepare for temple marriage. *Ideas:* Be morally clean, respect and support the priesthood, pay tithing, practice the law of the fast, be honest, obey the Word of Wisdom, set a good example, maintain clean speech, pray regularly, honor parents, choose a worthy companion, obey all of God's commandments.

TEMPLE MARRIAGE PANEL:
With the bishop's help, gather together a panel to discuss temple marriage. Choose recently married couples, older couples, and a recently sealed together family. Have young women write questions ahead of time, asking the bishop to direct a few.

MARRIAGE MUSEUM:
Create a museum of potential marriage companions. Create life-size silhouettes of couples out of colored craft paper and display them on the wall. Divide young women into two teams and give them a marker.
1. Assign one group of young women to write on one silhouette positive traits for an eternal mate that would lead them to an eternal marriage. Assign the second group to write on another silhouette those traits that would lead them away from a temple marriage.
2. Have young women share their lists of ideas.

CHASTITY (PAINTING RIGHTEOUS HABITS PLANNER):
To Make: Print the pattern (shown right) from the *Personal Progress* CD-ROM*. Or, copy or print the pattern from the *Young Women Fun-tastic! Activities – Manual 2* book or CD-ROM (Lesson #37). *Color.

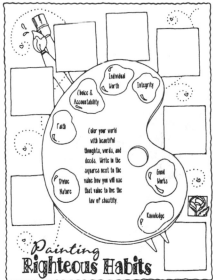

Activity: Using the *Painting Righteous Habits* planner, have each young women write what they consider righteous habits. Color the planner in the seven young women colors: Faith (white), Divine Nature (blue), Individual Worth (red), Knowledge (green) Choice and Accountability (orange), Good Works (yellow), and Integrity (purple). Tell young women that they can color their world with beautiful thoughts, words, and deeds, painting righteous habits daily. Have young women write in squares next to value how they will use that value to live the law of chastity.

CHOICE OF OREO COOKIES OR A BANQUET:
Prepare ahead of time a banquet of delightful food (e.g., pizza, salad, apple pie), and place under a tablecloth. Place a plate of Oreo cookies on top of the tablecloth. Tell young women that they can have an Oreo cookie *now* or wait for the treat that is under the tablecloth. Hint that what is under the tablecloth is much better than an Oreo, but they have to trust you. We have to trust our leaders, parents, etc., that saving intimacy until after marriage is a treat worth waiting for. After awhile uncover the tablecloth to serve young women the banquet (but not the Oreos). Then

All images shown in this book can be printed in color or black and white from the Young Women Fun-tastic! Personal Progress Motivators CD-ROM.

87

after they eat, take the Oreo cookies and crush them in front of them telling them that Satan wants you to be satisfied with immediate pleasure, e.g., the Oreo cookies, but it doesn't last. Heavenly Father wants us to wait for the banquet (having a sacred and eternal love), the relationship that is worth waiting for. Talk about Satan's temptations.

PANEL DISCUSSION (OBSERVING ONLY THE OUTWARD APPEARANCE (PACKAGING) CAN BE DECEIVING): (See the *Guest Daters—Dating Panel Discussion* on the following page.) Have a panel discussion to talk about dating relationships that help you learn the true character of that person. Talk about meeting a guy with a testimony one without a testimony, and how they can find their true character, and how "you can't judge a book by it's cover" (you need to look deeper). *Object Lesson:* Have young women unwrap some gifts. Wrap the gifts in a variety of plain and fancy, e.g., an old shoe, and a temple recommend, a *TV Guide,* a *The New Era* magazine, etc. Compare these with a guy who is not particularly handsome to them but could have great qualities they want eternally and to not overlook them.
Panel: Have priesthood leaders choose young men for the panels. Direct questions to the panel to learn how young women can bring out the spiritual side of a guy and learn what he is really like Questions: How can a girl tell if the guy will treat her with respect? How can she tell if he likes her for her good qualities and her testimony? How can a girl say no to affection and still keep a guy's friendship? What are the qualities a girl should look for that are deeper than the outward appearance? How can she find or bring out these inner qualities?

MY BIG DATING DECISIONS POSTER:
To Make: Print the pattern (shown left) from the *Personal Progress* CD-ROM*. Or, copy or print the pattern from the *Young Women Fun-tastic! Activities – Manual 3* book or CD-ROM (Lesson #35). *Color and cut out and glue part A to part B.
Activity: Young women can use this *Big Dating Decisions* poster to serve as reminders as they make their big dating decisions. Remind young women that each dating decision can impact her eternal life in the celestial kingdom with Heavenly Father and Jesus. To motivate eternal dating decisions, read the poster and the following scriptures: Jacob 6:11, and 2 Nephi 2:27-29 and 10:23.

DATE FOR MR. RIGHT:
Talk to young women about dating each young man as if their dates would someday be on video for their future mates to see. Tell them to date with the real purpose in mind (eternal marriage), to date as though their future posterity (children) were watching.
List Pitfalls to Avoid: Single dates, being alone with the opposite sex, dating nonmembers, dating someone who has different values, etc. Observe how their date treats his mother (a reflection on how he will someday treat his wife), observe how he feels about the Church, a mission, etc. Have

All images shown in this book can be printed in color or black and white from the Young Women Fun-tastic! Personal Progress Motivators CD-ROM.

88

young women ask themselves whether he is polite and considerate, what he likes to do with his time, etc.

Sneak Preview: Ahead of time (a week earlier) have the young men write down anonymously their ideal girl (what they like and don't like in a date or future mate).

REVIEW L.D.S. BOOKS ON DATING:

• Videos and recordings of dating and future choices are available at the Church Distribution Center and L.D.S. bookstores.

• Have a check-out system where each young woman can review these privately during the week if time does not allow you to show them all.

GUEST DATERS—DATING PANEL DISCUSSION:

(See the other Panel Discussion of the previous page).

Invite young men of dating age from another ward or stake to come and talk about dating. Ask them to talk about moral dating choices and how young people can avoid intimate situations. Have young women prepare questions in advance.

Sample Questions: What do you look for when you ask a girl out for a date? How can you tell if a girl has high standards? How do you like a girl to act on a date? What should or shouldn't a girl wear on a date? How does a girl say no to a kiss? How can a girl say no to physical advances? If a girl likes you but doesn't want to kiss on the date, how can she keep your mind off the kiss? How can a girl show you she likes you without kissing? What does a girl need to do to earn your respect? Do you like a girl to ask you out? If so, how should she ask you out without seeming aggressive? Do you like girls to flirt with you? How can she flirt with you without appearing too bold? What kinds of activities make dating fun? What date activities help you to get to know a girl better? How do you rate a girl? What do you look for? How should a girl show interest in you?

THE KEYS TO VIRTUOUS CHOICES VOTING BALLOT:

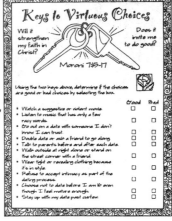

To Make: Print the pattern (shown right) from the *Personal Progress* CD-ROM*. Or, copy or print the pattern from the *Young Women Fun-tastic! Activities – Manual 1* book or CD-ROM (Lesson #36). *Color.

Activity: Tell young women that Heavenly Father has given us the keys to determine good from evil. Read Moroni 7:15-17. Using the *Keys to Virtuous Choices* voting ballot have young women read the choices and vote "good" or "bad" by checking the box. They can use the following keys to determine their answer: "Does it invite me to do good? Will it strengthen my faith in Christ?"

CHASTITY TALK AND CHASTITY CHOICES:

Bishops are very good at talking on this subject; so are their wives. Seminary teachers are also good resources. After a guest speaker, help young women project themselves into the future to look at choices they will make. Compare dating a boy who is good (chaste), and to dating a boy who is unchaste. Talk about group dates as opposed to single dating. Talk about the daily spiritual nourishment needed to help you make chaste choices.

HELP YOUNG WOMEN HELP YOUNG MEN PREPARE FOR THE TEMPLE:

Have young women read the pamplets: *Aaronic Priesthood: Fulfilling Our Duty to God* for the *Deacon, Teacher*, and *Priest* to learn of their values and goals. This way they can support them and help them prepare for a mission. Young women can set their own standards accordingly, helping them prepare and live worthy to attend the temple.

In the puzzle you must find and circle 18 things that will keep you out of the quicksand (Satan's traps) and on the right trail (chastity) in your journey through the jungle (world). If you stumble into the quicksand cross out the word before you start to circle! The word or word groups are read from left to right or backwards, right to left.

CAUTION! IT'S A JUNGLE OUT THERE! QUICKSAND BLACKOUT PUZZLE:

To Make: Print the pattern (shown left) from the *Personal Progress* CD-ROM*. Or, copy or print the pattern from the *Young Women Fun-tastic! Activities – Manual 2* book or CD-ROM (Lesson #33). *Color.

Activity:

1. Tell young women that the quicksand in the jungle of life is not easily seen. Satan camouflages evil, making it appear good and right. He sets traps and pits, like quicksand, all around us. If we get too close we can fall into them. Sometimes youth want to try something for themselves to see what it feels like, or they feel they can handle a situation and just go in part way. But even putting a toe into the deadly sand, letting down one's guard, can pull them in deeper until they are trapped in his powerful quicksand trap.

2. Have young women color and complete the puzzle to avoid Satan's traps and stay on the right trail.

ANSWERS starting top to bottom:

Quicksand Traps: masturbation, necking, dirty jokes, staying out late, petting, pornography, impure thoughts, immodesty, fornication, homosexuality, R-rated movies.

Chastity Trail: Enjoy group activities, listen to leaders' counsel and uplifting music, have virtuous thoughts, say prayers, seek true friendship, read scripture, say no, use clean speech, obey parents.

3. See the following "It's a Jungle Out There! Quicksand Traps" activity.

IT'S A JUNGLE OUT THERE! QUICKSAND TRAPS:

Set up a jungle scene with brown paper in the center to represent quicksand. Place a nice lounge chair with an umbrella with an intriguing drink on top of the quicksand. Take young women through the jungle scene and end up focusing on the lounge chair scene. Tell young women that below the chair is quicksand. They would naturally stay away from quicksand if they knew it was there. But Satan's traps are often disguised by trees in the jungle or in our lives by attractive objects or words that entice. Talk about Satan's quicksand traps to pull you under into necking, petting, intimacy, and sex. If we put our toe in the quicksand, we are tempted to go further until our feet and legs are stuck, and soon we are sitting in the quicksand. Before we realize it, we are up to our necks in Satan's trap. Have young women sit down and write questions on slips of paper and place

*All images shown in this book can be printed in color or black and white from the *Young Women Fun-tastic! Personal Progress Motivators* CD-ROM.

90

them in a box. Have leaders and young women talk about questions and how to avoid quicksand traps. Plan what to say in situations where it may be difficult to say no (e.g., at a party if alcohol is offered and we drink, we can then easily lose control). Heavenly Father reads or knows our thoughts but Satan does not have that power. Satan can only read our actions. If we give in a little, he tempts us further. Don't give him control by letting go of your values.

HUM A HYMN HUMMINGBIRD POSTER:

To Make: Print the pattern (shown right) from the *Personal Progress* CD-ROM*. Or, copy or print the pattern from the *Young Women Fun-tastic! Activities - Manual 1* book or CD-ROM (Lesson #34). *Color.
Activity: Encourage women to select a hymn they would like to memorize that they can hum when they are tempted with unvirtuous thoughts. Write the words to the hymn on this poster. Learn the scripture found in D&C 121:45 found on the poster.

CHOOSE YOUR WEAPON AGAINST IMMORAL THOUGHTS:
Tell young women to choose their weapon (a poem, thought, picture, song, or hymn) that helps them fight immoral thoughts and bring it with them. Have some great music, poetry, paintings that inspire, etc., ready and on hand. Be sure to have a picture of the Savior. Talk about inspiring thoughts, pictures, songs, or hymn. Share these with each other and enjoy them. Express your love and concern for these wonderful young women and how you want them protected. Remind them of their responsibility to their future spouse and children to stay worthy and clean.

DART WEAPON THROWING CONTEST TO FIGHT TEMPTATION:
Talk about pitfalls and temptations in dating that may lead to immorality. Write some of these temptations and challenges on small balloons (already blown up), then tape these onto a large poster. Talk about the fiery darts Satan sends out to tempt us (Ephesians 6:16). Divide into two teams to compete and throw darts to pop the balloon temptations. (Ahead of time tape a "FAITH" tag on each dart.) Say, "We can have our 'faith' darts ready to fight temptation."

DATING AND GROUP ACTIVITIES (GROUP TROUPERS! ACTIVITY IDEAS NOTEPAD):

To Make: Print the pattern (shown right) from the *Personal Progress* CD-ROM*. Or, copy or print the pattern from the *Young Women Fun-tastic! Activities - Manual 1* book or CD-ROM (Lesson #31). *Color.
Activity: Make several copies of the *Group Troupers! Activity Ideas* page to create a notepad to write wholesome activities with friends and dates ideas. Have a brainstorm to come up with ideas. *Ideas:* ❀ make your own movie ❀ write your own books ❀ put on your own theater ❀ take children on an outing e.g., the zoo or a children's museum ❀ have a formal dinner ❀ visit hospitals or shut-ins ❀ walk the neighborhood's dogs ❀ watch a ball game ❀ take a bus ride ❀ go bike riding ❀ go bowling ❀ go swimming ❀ go ice

*All images shown in this book can be printed in color or black and white from the *Young Women Fun-tastic! Personal Progress Motivators* CD-ROM.

skating ❀ go dancing ❀ go roller skating ❀ play bingo or board games (e.g., Monopoly), or card games (e.g., Skipbo) ❀ have a mixed-up holiday party ❀ have an un-birthday and bring white elephant (used gifts) ❀ have a family party ❀ have a picnic and go on a hike ❀ have the boys give a cooking demo to the girls and then the girls give a cooking demo to the boys ❀ put on a neighborhood garage sale ❀ organize and carry out a service project ❀ play games with the neighborhood children in the park ❀ read books to children ❀ read a book together ❀ plant or weed a garden ❀ hold a sports competition ❀ have a pie eating contest (young women bake pies and young men compete to eat them); then serve pies with ice cream on top ❀ have homemade ice cream and a crazy cookie bake; hand churn ice cream and have youth bring crazy treats to decorate frosted cookies.

HOST A DANCE:

Young women can host a theme dance with the works (dance instructors, food, and disc jockey).
❀ *Dance Theme #1 Western* (square dance, line dancing, or swing; have Kentucky Fried Chicken box lunches, apple bobbing, bales of hay, and western wear).
❀ *Dance Theme #2 Ballroom* (dress formal; have a formal dinner).
❀ *Dance Theme #3 Fifties* (dance to 50s oldies, e.g., Beatles, Beach Boys, Elvis, Jan and Dean; have hamburgers, fries, malts with whipped cream and a cherry on top).
❀ *Dance Theme #4 Disco Fever* (disco and Grease music, with a John Travolta and Olivia Newton-John dancing contest; have pizza, root beer floats).
❀ *Dance and Movie Theme #5 Roaring Twenties* (show the movie *Thoroughly Modern Millie* and make raspberry ice cream because in the movie Millie's friend says "raspberries!"). To make ice cream mix vanilla ice cream with frozen raspberries, adding milk as you blend in a blender.
❀ *At All Dances:* Have instructors present to teach dance steps. Give boys even numbers and girls odd numbers and place them in a drawing bowl for girls and one for boys. Have the girls draw a boy's number to choose a partner, and then boys choose a girl's number the next time. Let them choose a partner for a contest and award prizes.

CHOICE AND ACCOUNTABILITY
— VALUE EXPERIENCE #7: MAKE MONEY COUNT

MONEY MOTTOS AND SPENDING LIST TO PLACE IN WALLET:
To Make: Print the patterns (shown left) from the *Personal Progress* CD-ROM*. Or, copy or print the patterns from the *Young Women Fun-tastic! Activities – Manual 2* book or CD-ROM (Lesson #46).
*Color, cut out, and glue pieces back-to-back.
Activity: Give out the money motto (on one side) and *My Money Goals* planner (on the other side), and the *Do Not Forget . . . Stay Out of Debt* card to each young woman. Have them fill in the planner listing their money goals and laminate. They can enclose these in their wallet or purse as goal reminders. Talk about the responsibilities of finances and how to stay out of debt.

*All images shown in this book can be printed in color or black and white from the
Young Women Fun-tastic! Personal Progress Motivators CD-ROM.

92

WANTS AND NEEDS BUDGET PLAN:

Step #1: Have someone from an average household talk about how she budgets her time and money to make things work, to avoid debt, and to live within her means. Talk about the peace that can come into a home between husband and wife if they live within their means.

Step #2: Review books on how to budget.

Step #3: Divide young women into two groups, giving each group some play money. Ask them to figure a typical family budget and show where the money goes. Seeing a budget is believing. Have them start out with an average monthly income amount written on a card. Have them write on separate card their wants and needs, listing each expense on a different card. Have them lay the cards out on the table with the money next to the cards that they have budgeted for in that month's budget. Lay the other cards out also and talk about wants and needs.

Step #4: Talk about living within your means, cutting back and planning ahead, e.g., Christmas, birthdays, school clothes. Give the girls an envelope and suggest they place money in the envelope for things they are saving for. Have them write on the envelope things they want and prioritize these. Suggest they window shop (look for items without taking their money), then returning days later to make the purchase they really want or need.

Step #5: Review the *Pending Spending* activity below (which mentions tithing).

PENDING SPENDING:

Talk about ways you can put off spending to focus on priorities. Help young women picture themselves in the future starting a family on a budget. Help them visualize themselves in a budget-tight environment now, so that when they are in college and/or married, they can spend wisely.

❀ *Ideas:* $ Place money earned in an envelope labeled "Pending Spending," until they can take out tithing and savings; divide the balance of the money into envelopes to plan for upcoming events and purchases. $ Plan ahead where your money will be spent, e.g., gifts, greeting cards, vacation, or clothes. $ Plan ahead for birthdays, holidays, and special days to purchase gifts. $ Save for a mission and college. $ Place this money in a savings account and learn what interest can do.

BUDGET BRAINSTORM POSTER:

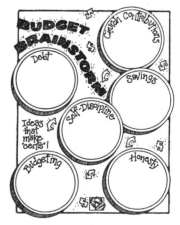

To Make: Print the pattern (shown right) from the *Personal Progress* CD-ROM*. Or, copy or print the pattern from the *Young Women Fun-tastic! Activities - Manual 3* book or CD-ROM (Lesson #46). *Color.

Activity: Say to young women, "A penny for your thoughts," and hand them a penny to hold as you brainstorm about budget ideas. Young women can take ideas home to post in their room, or they can write ideas in their journals about money management. Use the *Budget Brainstorm* poster to jot down ideas that make "cents." *Ideas that Make "Cents" (Sense):*

(1) Church Contributions (pay tithes and offerings first and blessings will come). (2) Debt (live within your income). (3) Savings (live within your earnings and put something away for a rainy day). (4) Self-Discipline (do without that which you cannot pay for). (5) Budgeting (plan money management to avoid debt). (6) Honesty (always ask, Is it right?).

*All images shown in this book can be printed in color or black and white from the
Young Women Fun-tastic! Personal Progress Motivators CD-ROM.

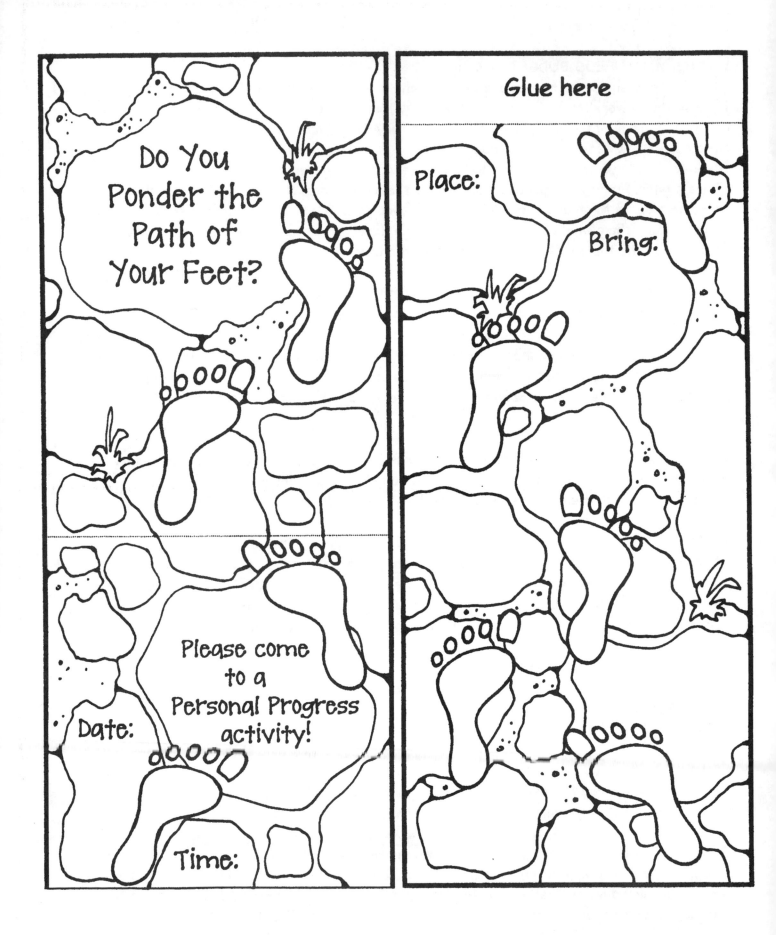

You Made the Choice to Step In the Right Direction

Certificate of Achievement
Awarded to

_____

for achieving your Choice and Accountability
Personal Progress goals!

_____   _____
Young Women Leader   Date

You Made the Choice to Step In the Right Direction

Certificate of Achievement
Awarded to

_____

for achieving your Choice and Accountability
Personal Progress goals!

_____   _____
Young Women Leader   Date

A Daughter of God Can Make Wise Decisions and Solve Problems

Choice and Accountability — Value Experience #1:

SEARCH AND PONDER:

1 Nephi 15:8, 2 Nephi 32:3, Alma 34:19-27
Ether 2-3, and Doctrine and Covenants 9:7-9

I Want to Make Wise Personal Decisions Such As:

Choosing Good Friends: _____

_____

Being Kind to Others: _____

_____

Getting up on Time: _____

_____

Other Decisions: _____

_____

I have followed a pattern of regular scripture study and prayer
to receive help in making these personal decisions. What I Did:

_____

_____

Choosing Standards of Righteous Behavior

Choice and Accountability – Value Experience #2:

SEARCH AND PONDER:

the pamphlet *For the Strength of Youth*

The standards of righteous behavior the pamphlet outlines:

STANDARDS: Why Each Standard is Important:

_____

_____

_____

_____

I Chose One of the above Standards I Need to Improve
And Worked on it Consistently for Three Weeks:

Standard: _____

Week #1: ___ Week #2: ___ Week #3: ___

How I improved my life by living this standard:

_____

_____

_____

Ideas: Be selective about television, music, books, and other
media, improve modesty, speech, or honesty.

I'm sharp! I'm sharp! I'm sharp! I'm sharp!

Hop to it! Agency Actions

Choice and Accountability — Value Experience #3:
SEARCH AND PONDER:

2 Nephi 2 and Doctrine and Covenants 82:2-10

With My Parent or Young Women Leader I Discussed Blessings of Agency:

_____

_____

And Responsibilities of Agency:

_____

_____

_____

The Consequences of My Choices and Actions:

_____

_____

_____

_____

_____

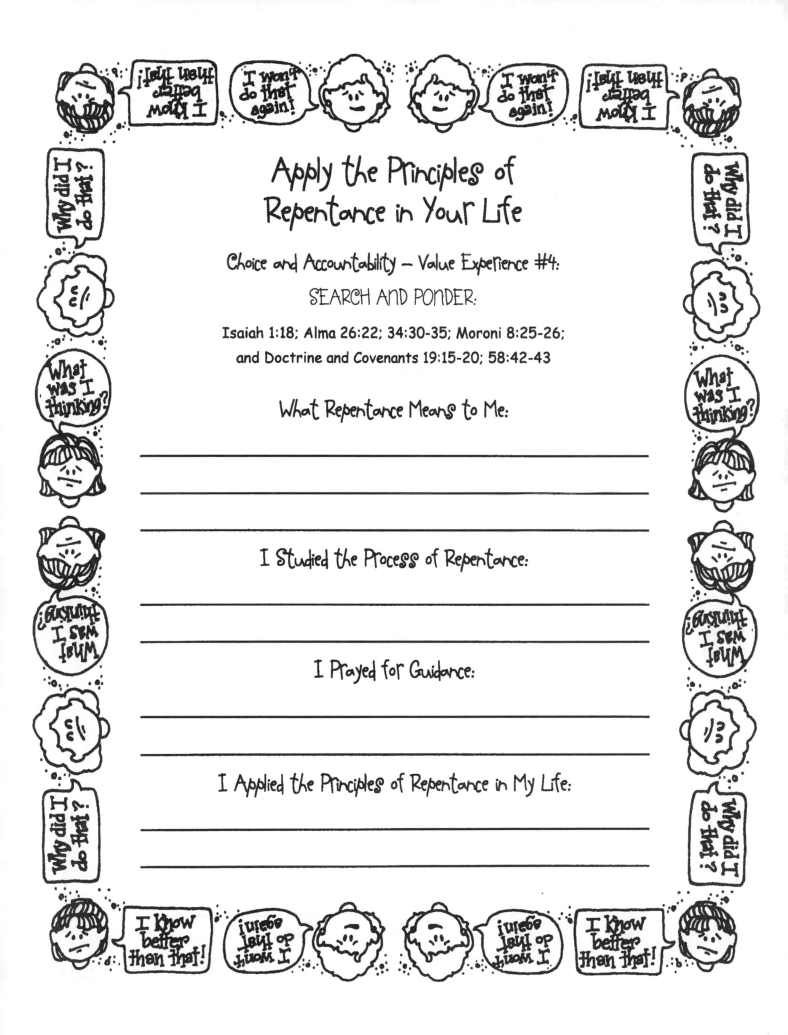

Apply the Principles of Repentance in Your Life

Choice and Accountability – Value Experience #4:
SEARCH AND PONDER:

Isaiah 1:18; Alma 26:22; 34:30-35; Moroni 8:25-26;
and Doctrine and Covenants 19:15-20; 58:42-43

What Repentance Means to Me:

_____

_____

I Studied the Process of Repentance:

_____

_____

I Prayed for Guidance:

_____

_____

I Applied the Principles of Repentance in My Life:

_____

_____

Learn about the Holy Ghost

Choice and Accountability – Value Experience #5:

SEARCH, PONDER, and DISCUSS:

Ezekiel 36:26-27; John 14:26; 16:13; Galatians 5:22-25;
2 Nephi 32:5; Moroni 10:4-5; and Doctrine and Covenants 11:12-14

How the Holy Ghost Can Help Me Make
Good Decisions in My Daily Life:

_____

_____

_____

_____

_____

I Have Made an Effort to Pray and Live Worthy of the
Companionship of the Holy Ghost. My Thoughts and Feelings:

_____

_____

_____

_____

Preparing to Enter the Temple

Choice and Accountability – Value Experience #6:

SEARCH AND PONDER:

the *Young Women Theme*
(on page 5 of the Personal Progress booklet)

After Reading the Young Women Theme I Discovered:

Who I am: _____

_____

What I am supposed to do: _____

_____

_____

Why I am to do these things: _____

_____

What I will do each day to be morally clean and worthy to enter the temple in the following areas:

Modesty: _____

Dating: _____

Media: _____

Making Your Money Count

Choice and Accountability — Value Experience #7:

SEARCH and PONDER:

Moses 4:1-4, 7:32, and 2 Nephi 9:51

We have the agency to make our own choices.

Spend our money for things of worth.

I will establish a pattern for wise money management by making and following a budget for savings and spending my money, including the payment of tithing.

Budget for Savings: _____

_____

Budget for Spending: _____

_____

Budget for Tithing (10%): _____

_____

I Have Tried to Live Within this Budget for Three Months:

Month #1: _____ Month #2: _____ Month #3: _____

MY PRIORITIES: Meet My Most Important Needs
Before Satisfying My Wants:

Important Needs (prioritized):	Wants:

Choice and Accountability
Value Project Planner

My Project Is:

_____

_____

_____

Steps to Carry Out My Project:

1. _____
2. _____
3. _____
4. _____
5. _____
6. _____
7. _____
8. _____

How I Felt about the Project:

_____

_____

How My Understanding of Choice and Accountability
Increased with this Project:

_____

_____

_____

Midweek Motivational Activities:

Value: Good Works
Theme: We Help Others and Build the Kingdom Through Righteous Service

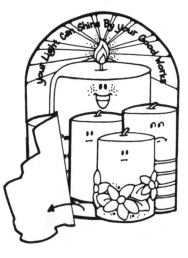

Invitation and Certificates: (1) *Copy the invitation and certificate (pages 115-116) for each young woman. (2) *Color and cut out images and fill in details. (3) To make invitation, fold and glue tabs to the back of the invitation. Deliver a week ahead. (4) See #5 below to distribute certificate.

Goal Planning and Sharing: You'll need a *copy of the Good Works Value Experience #1-7 planners and the Good Works Value Project Planner (pages 117-124) for each young woman.

DISTRIBUTE FORMS AND HAVE ONE OR MORE ACTIVITIES FROM THE FOLLOWING PAGES "FUN WAYS TO TEACH VALUES":

1. Tell young women that we can help others and build the kingdom through righteous service. Read 3 Nephi 12:16 (shown on page 47 in the Personal Progress booklet).

2. Give each young woman a set of Good Works Value Experience #1-7 planners and a Value Project Planner (sample shown left). Review each planner #1-7 titles, e.g., #1: "Learn Why Service is a Gospel Principle."

3. Suggest that they use the planners as worksheets to plan and carry out their goals and as a journal to record their experiences. When young women have passed off their goals, they can record these in their Personal Progress journal.

4. Suggest that they post the planners on the mirror as a reminder. When complete, store them in a looseleaf notebook or folder (see Introduction).

5. Award a Good Works certificate and a quilt block to young women who have achieved all their Good Works goals. See the Appendix to make the quilt.

Good Works

*All images shown in this book can be printed in color or black and white from the
Young Women Fun-tastic! Personal Progress Motivators CD-ROM.

Fun Ways to Teach Values:

Choose one or more of the following activities to motivate goal achievement.

GOOD WORKS — VALUE EXPERIENCE #1: SERVICE IS A GOSPEL PRINCIPLE

SERVE WITH STYLE FASHIONABLE MATCH GAME:

To Make: Print the pattern (shown right) from the *Personal Progress CD-ROM**. Or, copy or print the pattern from the *Young Women Fun-tastic! Activities – Manual 1* book or CD-ROM (Lesson #30). *Color and cut out.

Activity: Using the *Service with Style Fashionable Match Game* cards, help young women learn to serve with style. Read the set of cards and play a match game. Example, match: "You can be fashionable without spending a dime (card 1) and serve with a smile time after time (card 2)." Read 2 Corinthians 9:7. Play a match game using the cards.

SERVICE SING-ALONG:

Copy songs from the *Hymns* and frame them with borders. Have Young Women place them in their notebook behind the Good Works divider tab. Look for songs on page 425 under the "Service" topic. (For example, "Because I Have Been Given Much," page 219, or "Scatter Sunshine," page 230.)

SERVICE INVENTIONS:

Drive young women around the neighborhood and assign someone to take notes. List all they see that could be a service project. It's important that the girls do the noticing and noting. Go back to church or home, and decide which is most needful. Make assignments and plan the project(s), e.g., time and equipment needed and permission (if needed). Let the bishop know of the plan, and decide if they should keep it anonymous or not, and who should do what. Let young women lead on this; you sit back and advise a little. When it's their idea, the desire to serve is greater and the less you will need to motivate.

SERVICE PROJECT BRAINSTORM:

Have young women think up service ideas and vote on those you can do together. Then work to complete them.

*All images shown in this book can be printed in color or black and white from the *Young Women Fun-tastic! Personal Progress Motivators* CD-ROM.

105

Community Service
PROJECT PLANNER

Project I chose:_____

Type of Service:_____

Contact Person:_____ Phone:_____
Date of Project:_____ Time:_____
Location:_____
Who will be involved:_____
_____
_____
_____

Supplies Needed:_____

Notes:_____
_____
_____

Journal of My Experience:
_____
_____
_____
_____
_____
_____

COMMUNITY SERVICE PROJECT PLANNER:
To Make: Print the pattern (shown left) from the *Personal Progress* CD-ROM*. Or, copy or print the pattern from the *Young Women Fun-tastic! Activities – Manual 3* book or CD-ROM (Lesson #32). *Color.
Activity: Using the *Community Service Project Planner* encourage young women to take the time to serve others in their community and use this form to plan what they will do.

"GO THE EXTRA MILE" STRING LICORICE GAME:
To Create Game: Type up a list of service ideas gathered by young women or found in your local library or community service column in the local newspaper. Cut ideas into individual idea wordstrips. On 15 separate slips of paper, write numbers 1, 2, 3, 4, or 5. Fold all idea and number wordstrips in one container.

To Play Game:
1. Divide young women into two teams. Have teams take turns drawing a wordstrip from the pile of combined service ideas and numbers 1-5.
2. If they draw a service idea, tell others how they might perform this community service. They can then collect one string of licorice.
3. If they draw a number, e.g. "5," they name five service projects needed in a community, and collect five strings of licorice for their team.
4. The team with the most strings of licorice wins.
5. *Option:* Tie the licorice strings together, and at the end, instead of counting the number of strings, stretch it across the room to see who has the longest string. Say, "We will go the extra mile to serve in our community."
6. Ask young women to stretch the piece of licorice and think about stretching their talents as they serve.

GOOD WORKS — VALUE EXPERIENCE #2: PLAN FAMILY MEALS

PRETZEL PARTY:
Show young women how to make pretzels or fun-shaped rolls. Contact Rhodes Bake and Serve Company for a free booklet or demonstration.

HEALTHY HABITS SHARING:
Provide books on diet, nutrition, cookbooks, etc. (from the library). Photocopy a short piece from each book to share. Ask young women to share their ideas about eating healthful foods. Encourage young women to bring a copy of at least one healthful recipe they wish to prepare for their family.

All images shown in this book can be printed in color or black and white from the
Young Women Fun-tastic! Personal Progress Motivators CD-ROM.

HEALTHFUL FOOD TASTING TABLE:

Have young women bring a healthful dish to sample along with copies of recipes. Be sure they sign their name on the recipe. Bring the health food store to them with samples of carrot or green juice, soy products, sprouted bread, tofu/soy cheese, cream cheese and sour cream, healthy hot dogs (Tofu Pups), peanut butter without sugar, nuts, seeds, whole grains, soy margarine, wheat meat, protein powder, whole grain cereals, wheat grass, healing herbs, vitamins, essential oils, and more.

HEALTHFUL FOOD REFRIGERATOR MAGNETS:

To Make: Print the pattern (shown right) from the *Personal Progress* CD-ROM*. Or, copy or print the pattern from the *Young Women Fun-tastic! Activities – Manual 1* book or CD-ROM (Lesson #38). *Color, cut out, laminate, and glue a 1-inch magnet on the back of each.
Activity: Give each young woman a set of healthy food magnets to place on their refrigerator. Tell them that good nutrition is part of keeping the Word of Wisdom. If we can concentrate on high-nutrition rather than low-nutrition foods, we will be blessed, as it says in D&C 89:18-21.

PLANT SOME NUTRITIONAL IDEAS:

Show real plants or drawings of (1) a plant that has had little water, little sunlight, and no fertilizer, and (2) a plant that is healthy due to water, sunlight, fertilizer, etc. Explain that we are made of the same molecules, and our body requires certain nutrients to retain health. Some foods are poison to our bodies and some foods are medicine to our bodies. You can see people who are not caring for themselves properly and those who are. Some people look tired and pale, while others look bright and energetic! Talk about the story of Daniel as a youth in the king's court (Daniel 1:8-16). Explain that verse 12 *"pulse to eat"* means foods made of seeds, grains, etc.; see also Mosiah 9:8-9; D&C 89:14. Talk about the role of protein, carbohydrates, and fats. Note that the body needs balance.

SNACK ATTACK CURES:

Have young women share ideas for their favorite healthful snacks. Have them tell why this snack is good for them, e.g., an apple is 85% water and high in fiber ("nature's scrub brush"), celery calms the nerves and is also high in fiber.

*All images shown in this book can be printed in color or black and white from the
Young Women Fun-tastic! Personal Progress Motivators CD-ROM.*

107

GOOD WORKS — VALUE EXPERIENCE #3:
BEAR ONE ANOTHER'S BURDENS

SPREAD A LITTLE SUNSHINE SUNNY ACTION PLANNER:
To Make: Print the pattern (shown left) from the *Personal Progress CD-ROM**. Or, copy or print the pattern from the *Young Women Fun-tastic! Activities – Manual 2* book or CD-ROM (Lesson #49). *Color and cut out (cutting slits in between each sun ray to create 8 flaps).
ACTIVITY: Ask young women to identify a young woman at school or church who has a disability or special need, or who needs encouragement. Ask young women to reach out and include them in their activities, recognizing their special contributions and helping them participate in school, church, or community activities. Write on the *Sunny Action Planner* sun rays how you plan to spread a little sunshine in that person's life! When you complete your goal found on the sunray, cut off the sunray or fold it back and tape it to the back of the sun. *Ways to Spread a Little Sunshine:* Say hello, offer help, smile, be cheerful, sit by them, ask them places, find ways to help, ask others to help you help, be kind, call them by name, listen, talk about their interests, praise them, recognize their talents.

REACH OUT TO OTHERS HUMANITARIAN PROJECTS:
Get together with young men. Give young men the assignment to cut out small wooden blocks or animal shapes that young women can sand and paint. Go around and collect teddy bears and donate to your local fire department or police department. Make quilts or collect food donations for homeless shelters. Ask humanitarian representatives in ward or stake, city, or library for ideas. Make sure the less active young men and women are brought to this activity. Go out of your way to include all!

FRIEND-SHIP ANCHORS IN AN ETERNAL LIFEBOAT:
To Make: Print the patterns (shown left) from the *Personal Progress CD-ROM**. Or, copy or print the patterns from the *Young Women Fun-tastic! Activities – Manual 3* book or CD-ROM (Lesson #33). *Color and cut out ship and anchor wordstrips. Cut a slit in the back of the boat where indicated. Fold and glue boat on the rounded edge 1/4", leaving room for a pocket, and enclose wordstrips.
Activity: Talk about friendship being an anchor, something that holds our boat steady in times of trouble. Help young women learn ways to be an anchor or offer friendship and love to someone who needs support (especially if there is a less-active member or an investigator in the class). Challenge young women to take these *Friend-"ship" Anchor* wordstrips to serve as reminders. Ask young women to take turns pulling out a wordstrip (from one boat), and read the challenge. Tell why it is important, or share a personal experience. Read the following scriptures on friendship: 1 Samuel 16:7, Matthew 25:40, Romans 12:10, and Doctrine and Covenants 18:10. Encourage young women to do this activity with their family.

*All images shown in this book can be printed in color or black and white from the
Young Women Fun-tastic! Personal Progress Motivators CD-ROM.

108

PUT YOURSELF IN HER SHOES:

Have each young woman choose another young woman in the ward or at school, then talk to her and find out all about her. They can also talk to moms or sisters and find out their likes, dislikes, fears, and talents. Then when you meet, have young women tell the class about themselves as if they were the other girl, e.g., "I hate spiders. I have the coolest brother. My sister died at age three," etc. Then talk about how you can be better friends when you understand and feel empathy.

PAL PET PEEVES:

Brainstorm your likes and dislikes concerning friendships. Ideas will help young women in developing future friendships.

Make Friend-"ship" Banana Boats: Share with young women a banana boat treat they can create themselves. Cut a banana in half lengthwise. Dig out the center with a spoon and add chocolate chips, caramel, fudge, and miniature marshmallows. Top with two maraschino cherries to represent friends. Enjoy the treat as you talk about keeping their friends' eternal boats afloat by being a good influence.

GOOD WORKS — VALUE EXPERIENCE #4: TEACH FAMILY HOME EVENING
See Knowledge - Value Experience #7 for teaching ideas.
YOUNG WOMEN CAN SHARE THESE TESTIMONY IDEAS WITH THEIR FAMILY:

MY TESTIMONY SEEDS PACKET WITH
SCRIPTURE CARDS:

To Make: Print the pattern (shown right) from the *Personal Progress* CD-ROM*. Or, copy or print the pattern from the *Young Women Fun-tastic! Activities – Manual 1* book or CD-ROM (Lesson #26). *Color, cut out, fold, and glue together the seed packet, leaving the top open. Purchase seeds and enclose them before or after the writing activity.

Activity: Give a *Testimony Seeds* packet to each young woman to look up the scriptures on the packet to learn write ways they can gain a testimony; writing them on the packet. Challenge young women to go home and plant these seeds, water, and nourish them. Review the packet often to remind them that their testimony can grow as they read and ponder the scriptures each day.

TESTIMONY MATCH GAME:

Give young women two wordstrips and ask them to write a part, or a phrase, of their testimony on one wordstrip. Then have them write it again on the second wordstrip. Have them divide into two teams and play concentration by turning over two wordstrips to make a match. When a match is made, post one of each pair of wordstrips on the board or a poster. Afterwards, have young women take turns reading a testimony wordstrip and adding their own feelings to that testimony.

SHARING TIME TESTIMONY MEETING:

Have young women each present a short testimony to the Primary children during sharing time. They may create visuals or find visuals from the ward library that help them express their testimony. Their testimony might be on a gospel principle they feel strongly about (e.g., tithing, choosing the right, baptism, forgiveness, the Prophet Joseph Smith, Jesus Christ, the Holy Ghost, repentance, the Articles of Faith, Atonement, blessings, priesthood, faith, missionary work, Sacrament, the Word of Wisdom).

TESTIMONY TRACKER:

Have young women create a special notebook they can take to church meetings or put by their bed to note testimony ideas. As they learn of others' testimonies, ask them to try living certain gospel principles to increase their testimony. Say, "As you do this, record experiences that helped your testimony grow in this Testimony Tracker notebook."

TESTIMONY MEETING UNDER THE STARS:

Gather young women together and give them a piece of paper. Have them write their names on the paper, then show an appropriate church video that expresses what the Church is about (e.g., a video on the Savior or Joseph Smith and the Restoration). Afterwards, allow the young women to go to separate places and for 15 minutes write their feelings about the gospel. Tell them to write exactly what they feel. If they do not feel they are certain about gospel truths, ask them to write what they feel and know. Then gather the papers and read them without giving names (return them later). Help young women know they do have testimonies, some just beginning, others larger. Express that the size does not matter as much as the striving to know, grow, and continuing to nourish it. Express your own testimony and love for them. If possible, go to where you can all lie down on a blanket and look at the stars (or do something else that is inspiring). Pass out "starbursts" candy or other treat to reinforce the grand scheme of creation and our Heavenly Father's power and love.

FAMILY FUN ACTIVITIES BRAINSTORM:

FAMILY FUN ACTIVITY SACK:

To Make: Print the pattern (shown left) from the *Personal Progress* CD-ROM*. Or, copy or print the pattern from the *Young Women Fun-tastic! Activities – Manual 3* book or CD-ROM (Lesson #10). *Color and cut out sack label and wordstrips and enclose them in a zip-close bag. *Activity:* Place *Family Fun Activity Sack* label and wordstrips in a bag. Ask young women to motivate their family to fun activities by drawing these activities out of the sack to do for family home evening. To review what's in the sack, have young women take turns drawing wordstrips from one sack. Read them aloud. Encourage young women to invent their own ideas and place them on wordstrips to add to their *Family Fun Activity Sack.* Review the Five Ways to Create Memorable Moments on the label (detailed in Lesson #10 in the *Young Women Manual 3*).

*All images shown in this book can be printed in color or black and white from the
Young Women Fun-tastic! Personal Progress Motivators CD-ROM.

110

Family Fun Sack Brainstorm: Ask young women to write down their favorite family fun activities to share with the others. Type and photocopy their bright ideas to share.

Family Activity Show-and-Tell: Ask several young women to show others how to do their activity. They could bring games, have relay races, put on a play or skit, etc.

Have Parents Share Ideas: Have parents come and discuss ways to have a successful family home evening.

Family Home Evening Show-and-Tell: Ask young women to show ideas on family home evening. Look for the books and CD-ROMs by Ross and King: *Home-spun Fun Family Home Evenings,* Vol. 1 and 2, *File Folder Family Home Evenings, Gospel Fun Activities,* and *Sharing Time.*

GOOD WORKS — VALUE EXPERIENCE #5: SHOW LOVE THROUGH SERVICE

SMALL ACTS OF KINDNESS:

Brainstorm and write down ideas of small acts of kindness they can do for others. Encourage them to look into the mirror and say, "Mirror, mirror, tell me true. Is His image in my countenance too?" As they say this, they can look at the list and perform small acts of kindness.

Ideas: ❀ a sweet anonymous note ❀ a phone call to someone less active ❀ a smile ❀ breakfast in bed for a family member ❀ a friendly touch ❀ a compliment ❀ find out someone's favorite goody, make it for them, and deliver with a smile

BISHOP: THANKS A BUNCH! SUNFLOWERS IN A POT:

To Make: Print the pattern (shown right) from the *Personal Progress* CD-ROM*. Or, copy or print the pattern from the *Young Women Fun-tastic! Activities – Manual 2* book or CD-ROM (Lesson #11). *Color and cut out flowers and label. Glue label on a pot, and flowers on wooden dowels or long straws. Fill pot with treats.

Activity: Create a *Thanks a bunch!* flower pot that young women can give to the bishop, filled with sunflower thank-you notes. Give each young woman a flower where they can write a thank you message on the front. When young women present the pot to the bishop, have them read their note and place their flower in the pot. *Note Ideas:* Thanks for: Helping us choose the right. Receiving revelation for the ward. Shaking hands. Helping members repent. Being a good example. Greeting with a smile. Encouraging us to pay tithing and fast offerings. Helping us be missionaries. Helping needy families. Giving interviews for the temple. Having a testimony. Being a friend. Visiting ward members. Helping with funerals. Supervising leaders. Praying and fasting for ward members. Counseling and helping with problems. Teaching the gospel.

COOK THE BISHOP HIS FAVORITE DESSERT:

Ask the bishop's wife what his favorite dessert is. Make, decorate, and deliver. For example, bake a pie and decorate the top, using frosting in a tube to create a man's shirt collar and tie. Present to the bishop.

BISHOP HONOR NIGHT:

Have the bishop's wife help plan and prepare the activity. Spotlight him, telling about his hobbies or things he likes to do and things she likes about him. Tell his favorite food and serve some. Involve his family.

HONOR THE ELDERLY:

Using the *Thanks a Bunch! Sunflowers in a Pot* activity ideas (shown above) to have young women spotlight their grandparents or an elderly friend.

GOOD WORKS — VALUE EXPERIENCE #6: GIVE SERVICE OUTSIDE FAMILY

See Good Works — Value Experience #1, 3, and 5 and Knowledge #5

GOOD WORKS — VALUE EXPERIENCE #7: MISSIONARY EXPERIENCE

GUESS WHO SHARED THE GOSPEL? PROPHETS CROSSMATCH:

To Make: Print the pattern (shown left) from the *Personal Progress CD-ROM**. Or, copy or print the pattern from the *Young Women Fun-tastic! Activities – Manual 3* book or CD-ROM (Lesson #21). *Color.

Activity: Remind young women of some of the prophets through the ages who shared the gospel of Jesus Christ with others. With this *Guess Who? Prophets Cross Match,* young women can read the scriptures and imagine what it would be like to be a prophet—who was sometimes the only one preaching the gospel. From this activity young women can learn ways they can prepare themselves to share the gospel with others.

CANOE CHATS:

Go on an imaginary or real canoe ride (on blankets or on water) with someone you would like to get to know better, Laurel with a Beehive, or Mia Maid with a Beehive. When you return, report one thing that impressed you about your partner. Talk about getting to know another person before you begin this activity, what to say, how to develop a friendship, and how to help another person feel comfortable around you. After young women have shared their comments about the canoe trip, talk about how they might fellowship a friend from another faith or someone recently baptized.

*All images shown in this book can be printed in color or black and white from the
Young Women Fun-tastic! Personal Progress Motivators CD-ROM.

112

SERVE FRIEND-"SHIP" SANDWICHES:

Make a half sandwich for the boat and place a toothpick in a slice of processed cheese for the sail. Tell young women to have courage as they sail into friendships with those who are not members of our faith. Think of where you would be today without the gospel and where others might be tomorrow if they had the gospel.

MISSIONARY FOR A DAY:

Have young women learn what a typical week is like in the life of a missionary. Plan a day or a few hours where they can sample it all. Ask sister missionaries to come and tell them what they do.
Ideas: Reading the scriptures together, going on splits with the missionaries, visiting member neighbors, asking questions about their friends, encouraging them to fellowship others, cooking healthy meals in a hurry, practicing social skills.

MISSIONARY PREP MIRROR MOTIVATORS:

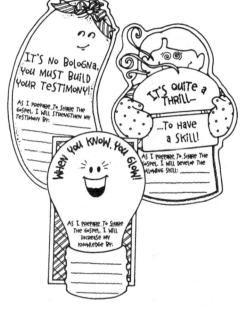

To Make: Print the patterns (shown right) from the *Personal Progress* CD-ROM*. Or, copy or print the patterns from the *Young Women Fun-tastic! Activities – Manual 2* book or CD-ROM (Lesson #19). *Color and cut out motivators.
Activity: Give each young woman a set of *Missionary Preparation Mirror Motivators* to challenging them to prepare to be a missionary. Have them fill in the blanks to set mission preparation goals and post on their mirror as a reminder.

SCHOOL DAZE AND MISSIONARY WAYS WORKSHOP:

Ask young women to divide into teams to discuss ways they can be a missionary at school. Encourage them to show how they can team up to fellowship and befriend a friend of another faith and less-active girls. They can put on a skit, write a poem, give ideas, make up situations, role play, or ask questions and talk about being a missionary.

MISSION PREP PARTY:

Give young women a mock missionary badge as they enter the room. Have experts in each area give a demonstration, teaching their valuable skills.
Ideas: Learn to iron; do laundry; sew on a button; make scones; lead music; introduce yourself; learn about facial expressions and eye contact; discuss dress, grooming, posture, and conversation.

MISSIONARY DISCUSSIONS TO ALL YOUNG WOMEN:

Have the missionaries in your area or a returned missionary give the discussions to all young women (over several evenings). Offer discussions #1-6 found in the *Uniform System for Teaching the Gospel* booklets. Discussions:

1. The Plan of Our Heavenly Father
2. The Gospel of Jesus Christ
3. The Restoration
4. Eternal Progression
5. Living a Christlike Life, and
6. Membership in the Kingdom.

All images shown in this book can be printed in color or black and white from the Young Women Fun-tastic! Personal Progress Motivators CD-ROM.

FRIENDSHIP SEMINAR:

As young women learn how to make friends and be a loyal friend, this will help them to become better missionaries. Have young women separate into different workshops with different young women or leaders sharing ideas on being a friend. Encourage young women to place questions about being a friend and finding friends in a question box, then read them aloud. Have the other young women and leaders respond to answer the questions.

Subjects to Discuss: How to Make a Friend: ❀ How to Keep a Friendship Going ❀ How to Know If That Person Wants to Be a Friend ❀ What If You Don't Like a Person ❀ How Do You Converse with a Friend ❀ How Do You Share the Gospel with a Friend

BOOK OF MORMON TESTIMONY AND SCRIPTURE UNDERLINING:

To Make: Print the pattern (shown left) from the *Personal Progress* CD-ROM*. Or, copy or print the pattern from the *Young Women Fun-tastic! Activities – Manual 2* book or CD-ROM (Lesson #20). *Color and cut out.

Activity: (1) Give each young woman a copy of the Book of Mormon and challenge her to read it if she hasn't already. (2) Have young women pray for a testimony and write their testimony of the Book of Mormon on the Come Unto Christ form. Glue this to the inside front of the Book of Mormon. (3) Have young women glue the scripture list to one of the front pages of the Book of Mormon and underline the selected scriptures in red pencil so investigator can turn right to the scriptures. (4) Give the Book of Mormon to a friend or the missionaries. Young women could include a photo of themselves.

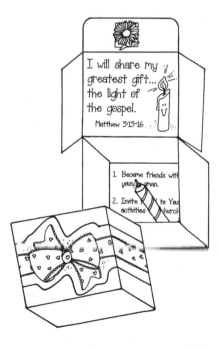

SHARE THE GOSPEL BRAINSTORM:

Have the full-time missionaries come and talk to the young women as a group about those in the area they wish to friendship/fellowship. Have the girls prepare questions, ideas, and concerns. Assign young women to fellowship certain young women who are of another faith or a recent convert, or to encourage young women who are less active.

LIGHT OF THE GOSPEL CANDLE GIFT BOX:

To Make: Print the pattern (shown left) from the *Personal Progress* CD-ROM*. Or, copy or print the pattern from the *Young Women Fun-tastic! Activities – Manual 1* book or CD-ROM (Lesson #20). *Color and cut out box and bow, fold, and glue together, leaving top flap open. Place a small birthday candle in box. Fold bow on box fold lines and glue at the bottom. Slide bow over box.

Activity: Create a gift candle box to present to each young woman to remind her of the three steps to sharing her greatest gift—the light of the gospel: (1) Become friends with a young woman. (2) Invite friend to Young Women activities and to church. (3) Invite friend to be taught by the missionaries. Read Matthew 5:15-16.

*All images shown in this book can be printed in color or black and white from the
Young Women Fun-tastic! Personal Progress Motivators CD-ROM.

114

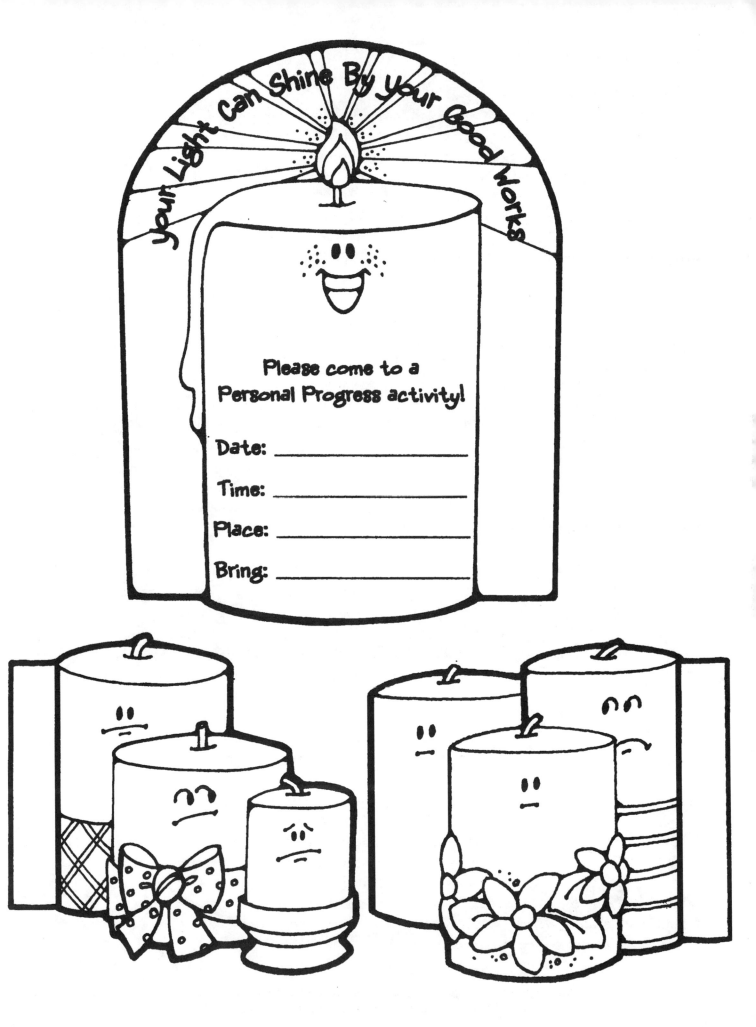

Your Light Can Shine By Your Good Works

Please come to a
Personal Progress activity!

Date: _____

Time: _____

Place: _____

Bring: _____

Your Good Works Are a Light to Others

Certificate of Achievement
Awarded to

_____

for achieving your Good Works
Personal Progress goals!

_____   _____
young Women Leader   Date

Your Good Works Are a Light to Others

Certificate of Achievement
Awarded to

_____

for achieving your Good Works
Personal Progress goals!

_____   _____
young Women Leader   Date

Learn Why Service is a Gospel Principle

Good Works – Value Experience #1:

SEARCH AND PONDER:

Matthew 5:13-16; 25:34-40; Galatians 6:9-10;

James 1:22-27; Mosiah 2:17; 4:26; and 3 Nephi 13:1-4

Why Service is a Principle of the gospel:

_____

_____

For Two Weeks I Recorded Quiet Acts of Service My Family Members or Others Performed and Acknowledged Them for Their Service:

Who: What:

_____

_____

_____

_____

_____

_____

Week #1: M __ T __ W __ T __ F __ S __ S __

Week #2: M __ T __ W __ T __ F __ S __ S __

Service Actions That Often Go Unnoticed: preparing meals, reading or listening to younger children, repairing clothing, helping a brother or sister.

Help Plan Family Meals
and Gather Together at Mealtime

Good Works – Value Experience #2:

For Two Weeks I helped plan my family's menus,

obtain food, and prepare part of the meals.

Week #1: M __ T __ W __ T __ F __ S __ S __

Week #2: M __ T __ W __ T __ F __ S __ S __

I Helped My Family Gather Together at Mealtimes
and this is what I learned:

_____

_____

_____

_____

_____

_____

Meals I Helped with:

Monday: _____   Tuesday: _____

Wednesday: _____   Thursday: _____

Friday: _____   Saturday: _____

Sunday: _____   Monday: _____

Tuesday: _____   Wednesday: _____

Thursday: _____   Friday: _____

Saturday: _____   Sunday: _____

Comfort, Help, and "Bear" One Another's Burdens

Good Works – Value Experience #3:

SEARCH AND PONDER:

Mosiah 18:7-10

Three Ways I Can Help Comfort Others and Bear their Burdens:

1. _____
2. _____
3. _____

I did the above three things and this is how I felt (how my attitude changed):

_____
_____
_____
_____
_____
_____
_____
_____
_____

Teach Family Home Evening
About a Gospel Subject

Good Works – Value Experience #4:

Gospel Subject: _____

Pictures Used: _____

Music: _____

Examples or Demonstrations in Lesson: _____

_____

Lesson:

_____

_____

_____

_____

_____

_____

_____

_____

_____

_____

_____

_____

Resource Used: Teaching, No Greater Call
(found at the ward/branch library)

Show Love Through Service

Good Works — Value Experience #5:

SEARCH AND PONDER:

Doctrine and Covenants 58:26-28

These are Ways a Young Woman or a Wife and Mother
Could Apply the Above Scripture in her Family:

_____

_____

_____

I Developed a Pattern of Service in My Life by
Choosing the Following Family Member I Can Help:

_____

Ways I Served Him/her and My Feelings about this Service:

_____

_____

_____

_____

I Served this Person for One Month (Circle the Days):
1 2 3 4 5 6 7 8 9 10 11 12 13 14 15 16 17
18 19 20 21 22 23 24 25 26 27 28 29 30

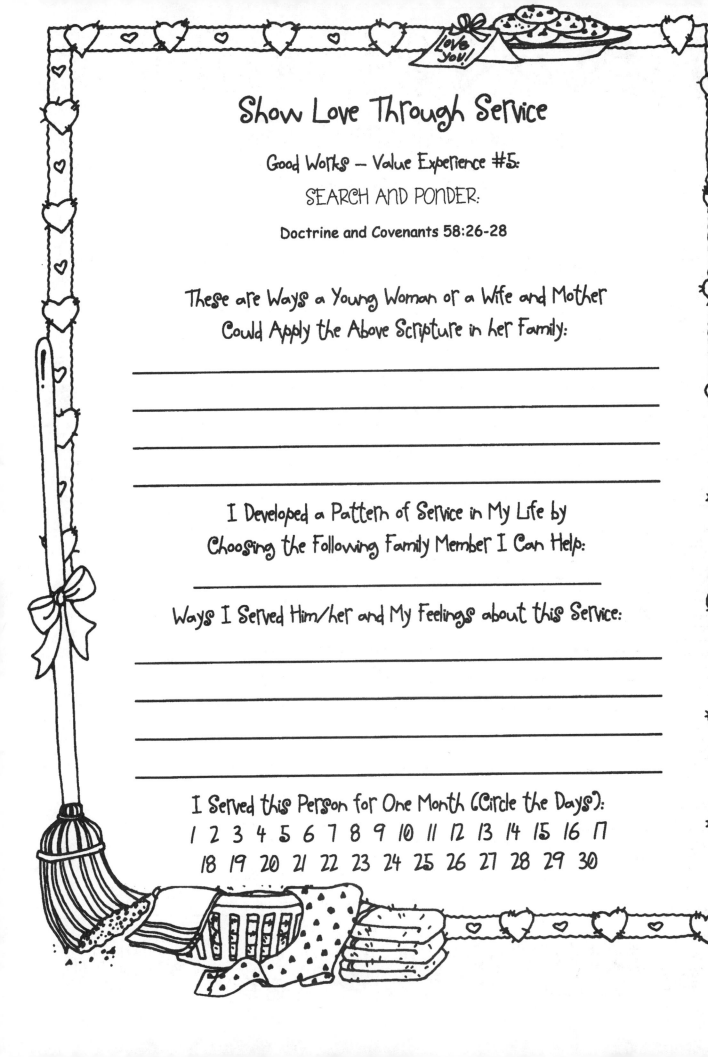

Give Service Outside Your Family

Good Works – Value Experience #6:

I spent at least three hours giving service as follows:

_____

_____

_____

Ask ward or branch Relief Society president or
community leader for service ideas.

Ideas are found on page 49 in the Personal Progress booklet.

Example: Babysit while parents attend the temple.

IDEAS: _____

_____

_____

_____

Reactions of the Person I Served:

_____

_____

Goals for Future Service Opportunities:

_____

_____

_____

Pray for a Missionary Experience

Good Works – Value Experience #7:

SEARCH AND PONDER:

Matthew 24:14; 28:19; and Doctrine and Covenants 88:81
"If we do not understand and willingly teach others the Restoration of the gospel of Jesus Christ through the Prophet Joseph Smith, who will?"
- Elder M. Russell Ballard, Quorum of the 12 Apostles,
October, 2000 General Conference

___ I prayed earnestly that I might have a missionary experience, to find those who are "honest in heart."

I Invited a Friend Who Is Not a Member or One Who Is less Active to Go with Me to a Church Meeting or Activity As Follows: _____

_____

_____

This Is How I Felt:

_____

_____

These Are My Future Missionary Goals:

_____

_____

_____

Good Works Value Project Planner

My Project Is:

_____

_____

_____

_____

Steps to Carry Out My Project:

1. _____
2. _____
3. _____
4. _____
5. _____
6. _____
7. _____
8. _____

How I Felt about the Project:

_____

_____

_____

How My Understanding of Good Works Increased with this Project:

_____

_____

Midweek Motivational Activities:
Value: Integrity
Theme: We Have Moral Courage to Choose Right Actions

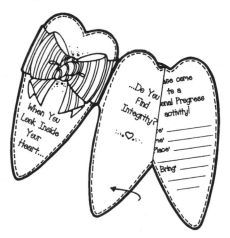

Invitation and Certificates: (1) *Copy the invitation and certificate (page 134) for each young woman. (2) *Color and cut out images and fill in details. (3) To make invitation, fold accordion style. Deliver a week ahead. (4) See #5 below to distribute certificate.

Goal Planning and Sharing: You'll need a *copy of the Integrity Value Experience #1-7 planners and the Integrity Value Project Planner (pages 135-142) for each young woman.

DISTRIBUTE FORMS AND HAVE ONE OR MORE ACTIVITIES FROM THE FOLLOWING PAGES "FUN WAYS TO TEACH VALUES":

1. Tell young women that we can have the moral courage to make our actions consistent with our knowledge of right and wrong. Read Job 27:5 (shown on page 54 in the Personal Progress booklet).

2. Give each young woman a set of Integrity Value Experience #1-7 planners and a Value Project Planner (sample shown left). Review each planner #1-7 titles, e.g., #1: *Strength of Youth Standards*.

3. Suggest that they use the planners as worksheets to plan and carry out their goals and as a journal to record their experiences. When young women have passed off their goals, they can record these in their Personal Progress journal, if desired.

4. Suggest that they post the planners on the mirror as a reminder. When complete, store them in a looseleaf notebook or folder (see Introduction).

5. Award a Integrity certificate and a quilt block to young women who have achieved all their Integrity goals. See the Appendix to make the quilt.

*All images shown in this book can be printed in color or black and white from the
Young Women Fun-tastic! Personal Progress Motivators CD-ROM.

Fun Ways to Teach Values:

Choose one or more of the following activities to motivate goal achievement.

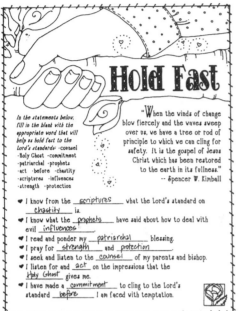

INTEGRITY — VALUE EXPERIENCE #1: STANDARDS FOR THE STRENGTH OF YOUTH
See also Choice and Accountability —
Value Experiences #2 and #6

HOLD FAST (TO THE STANDARDS) WORD FIND:
To Make: Print the pattern (shown left) from the *Personal Progress CD-ROM**. Or, copy or print the pattern from the *Young Women Fun-tastic! Activities – Manual 2* book or CD-ROM (Lesson #34). *Color.

Activity: Have young women do the *Hold Fast* word find to help them realize the importance of holding fast to the Lord's standards. Read the quote by Spencer W. Kimball. Have young women fill in the missing word to identify ways they can hold fast to the Lord's standards.

GOSPEL STANDARDS WORD FIND:
To Make: Print the pattern (shown left) from the *Personal Progress CD-ROM**. Or, copy or print the pattern from the *Young Women Fun-tastic! Activities – Manual 3* book or CD-ROM (Lesson #37). *Color.

Activity: Read John 14:27 *"My peace I give unto you: not as the world giveth."* Explain that Jesus sent us the Holy Ghost, the Comforter, to speak to our hearts and minds as we live the gospel standards. This is the peace that we need in this troubled world. Using the *Gospel Standards* word find, young women can review their gospel standards—how they are different from worldly philosophies, and how they (gospel standards) will bring them peace, as the Savior promised in this scripture.

1. Find and circle the gospel standards in the word find and highlight any that are of a special challenge to you.

2. Find the *Worldly Philosophies* word(s) found on the right; opposite the *Gospel Standard* column on the left. *Example:* "Astrology" (using the stars to pretend to tell fortunes) is opposite of our gospel standards of a "patriarchal blessing," where we receive direct revelation from our Heavenly Father as to our purpose and direction in this life. We also receive this direct revelation in our personal prayers, through the prophet, church leaders, and parents who are inspired to lead and guide us.

3. Unscramble the world philosophies and write them in the blank column on the right.

*All images shown in this book can be printed in color or black and white from the Young Women Fun-tastic! Personal Progress Motivators CD-ROM.

4. Discuss how, like the word scramble, worldly philosophies are confusing and misleading.
Answers: (astrology, pornography, immorality, harmful substances, civil marriage, divorce, and abortion).

5. From the highlighted gospel standards (see #1 above), challenge yourself to study these gospel standards in the scriptures, *The New Era* and *Ensign* Church magazines, and church books, learning the word of the Lord and his prophets until you feel secure and at peace with these standards.

Standards For the Strength of Youth Review:
Review these *Standards* in the Young Women Personal Progress booklet (pages 2-4). Ask young women to write their personal questions and put them in a box. Have the bishop or youth leader answer the questions during the next meeting.

INTEGRITY — VALUE EXPERIENCE #2: CHANGE IN BEHAVIOR

HARVESTING MY DESTINY GARDEN HABIT CHANGER:
To Make: Print the pattern (shown right) from the *Personal Progress* CD-ROM*. Or, copy or print the pattern from the *Young Women Fun-tastic! Activities – Manual 2* book or CD-ROM (Lesson #40). *Color.

Activity: Using the *Harvesting My Destiny Garden* young women can learn that by planting three tiny seeds of thought, they can overcome three bad habits and reap a harvest of good habits that will determine their eternal destiny.

1. Have young women write on the *Destiny Garden* habit changer three bad habits they wish to change e.g., lazy, selfish, bad moods.
2. Sow a good thought. Below the bad habit, they can write a positive thought that will change the bad habit. (e.g., If the habit is "laziness," write "I like to work," or if the habit is "selfishness," write, "I will think of others," or if the habit is "bad moods," write, "I will think happy thoughts.")
3. Write in the *Harvest Your Destiny Garden* section what each thought reaps (action, habit, character, and destiny).

IT'S TIME FOR A CHANGE! DIAPER BAG:
To Make: Print the pattern (shown right) from the *Personal Progress* CD-ROM*. Or, copy or print the pattern from the *Young Women Fun-tastic! Activities – Manual 2* book or CD-ROM (Lesson #47). *Color and cut out diaper and change cards. Fold diaper and glue back-to-back leaving the top open. Insert cards.

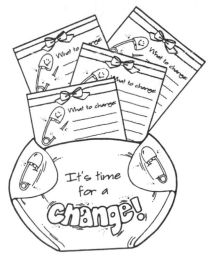

Activity: Make the *It's Time for a Change!* diaper and change cards. Young women can write on the cards what they want to change and how they will make these changes (e.g., your room, your friends, your hobbies, use of time, personal attitudes, types of media presentation, cleanliness).

*All images shown in this book can be printed in color or black and white from the
Young Women Fun-tastic! Personal Progress Motivators CD-ROM.

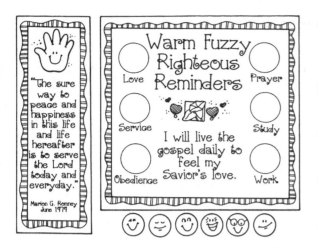

SERVICE BOOKMARK AND MIRROR MOTIVATOR:

To Make: Print the patterns (shown left) from the *Personal Progress* CD-ROM*. Or, copy or print the patterns from the *Young Women Fun-tastic! Activities – Manual 3* book or CD-ROM (Less. #3). *Color and cut out bookmark and *Warm Fuzzy Righteous Reminders*, leaving the happy faces attached. Glue six colored cotton balls or pom-poms above the six challenges.

Activity: The bookmark encourages young women to draw close to the Savior by serving him everyday. The *Warm Fuzzy Righteous Reminder* mirror motivator

shows six ways we can change our behavior to feel close to the Savior each day. Encourage young women to post the *Warm Fuzzy Righteous Reminders* poster on their mirror to remind them to practice the behaviors, then glue a smiling face sticker on top of cotton or pom-pom when the behavior is changed.

MY FUTURE FOCUS PLANNER:

To Make: Print the pattern (shown left) from the *Personal Progress* CD-ROM*. Or, copy or print the pattern from the *Young Women Fun-tastic! Activities – Manual 1* book or CD-ROM (Lesson #32). *Color.

Activity: Tell young women that they can focus on a positive future by making decisions about critical issues ahead of time. Using the *My Future Focus Planner* young women can write in the column on the right what they are willing to give up or willing to do to obtain what they want (column on the left).

DISCIPLINED DEMOS:

Ask young women to share their talents in a talent night or invite someone with a particular talent to come and tell how having discipline helped develop this talent. Tell young women that permissive or careless behavior brings loss of freedom and failure, while disciplined or correct behavior brings freedom or success. Encourage young women to develop their character by saying "no" to permissive or careless behaviors. Have young women write down (anonymously) something they struggle with (sleeping too much, telling lies, gossiping, not eating right, not exercising enough, not doing school work, not practicing music, etc.) Share an area that you need to work on, recognizing that we all have weaknesses. Place papers in a container and mix them up, then read them aloud and discuss them. Tell young women that the key to success is to let the Spirit of the Holy Ghost guide them. Challenge them to do this the rest of the week to help them cultivate disciplined behaviors. Follow up with their progress on Sunday.

*All images shown in this book can be printed in color or black and white from the *Young Women Fun-tastic! Personal Progress Motivators* CD-ROM.

128

INTEGRITY — VALUE EXPERIENCE #3: COURAGE TO SHOW INTEGRITY

TRUE TO THE FAITH TOOLS CROSSMATCH JOURNAL:

To Make: Print the pattern (shown right) from the *Personal Progress* CD-ROM*. Or, copy or print the pattern from the *Young Women Fun-tastic! Activities – Manual 1* book or CD-ROM (Lesson #35). *Color.

Activity: Tell young women that they can be true to the faith in spite of worldly pressures. Using the *True to the Faith Tools* journal, have young women list five worldly pressures in the left column. Have them draw a line to the tool or tools that would help them overcome each worldly pressure, e.g.: parents, good friends, scriptures, the Holy Ghost, church leaders, and family members. Have them write about blessings they would receive from overcoming each pressure.

CATERPILLARS:

Have pictures of beautiful butterflies everywhere. Try to find a chart of how a caterpillar becomes a butterfly. Explain how it struggles for a long time to emerge from the cocoon. Tell the story of a young lady who was watching this process and decided to help. It looked like the caterpillar was having a hard time coming out of its cocoon, so she gently peeled open the cocoon a little for the butterfly. As she watched over the next few days, it came out more easily, but its body was much larger than normal and its wings were limp and frail. It could not fly but only wiggle and flop along the ground. This is because the butterfly must work hard to gain its freedom. The pressure to squeeze out of the tight cocoon pushes blood to its wings and completes the process. In the same way, pressure can make us strong. We can take the easy road or we can show discipline and courage and persistence and become much more! Make butterfly or caterpillar cookies that young women can frost and decorate to take home or make a butterfly cake (cut wings out of sheet cake). (Option: make a long caterpillar with Hostess Snowballs and licorice for the antennae.) See *The New Me!* Changing Caterpillar butterfly poem poster in *Fun-tastic! Young Women Activities*—Manual 3, Lesson #42—(shown and detailed below).

CHANGING CATERPILLAR POEM POSTER:

To Make: Print the pattern (shown right) from the *Personal Progress* CD-ROM*. Or, copy or print the pattern from the *Young Women Fun-tastic! Activities – Manual 3* book or CD-ROM (Lesson #42). *Color.

Activity: Ask young women to place *The New Me* poster on their wall to read and remind them to stay close to Spirit of the Holy Ghost, who will guide them in making changes. Also see the *Caterpillars* activity above.

*All images shown in this book can be printed in color or black and white from the
Young Women Fun-tastic! Personal Progress Motivators CD-ROM.

LEARN THAT "PRACTICE MAKES PROGRESS:"
Encourage young women to keep going, no matter how hard the task. Tell them that each time they do something that is difficult, it becomes easier the next time. So take the plunge! Challenge them to make a list of difficult tasks and set goals to achieve these tasks.

CHANGE IS IMPORTANT TO FIND HAPPINESS:
Tell young women that our life changes daily in many ways. The Lord knows what is coming. We do not need a crystal ball or psychic reading to be prepared for the future. The Holy Ghost will prompt us and guide us if we are prayerful and listen to the promptings. This way we can find true happiness in making our daily decisions.

1. *Learn About Change.* Read stories about young men and women from the *New Era* who made changes in their lives. Show *Mormonad* posters (available at the Church Distribution Center), e.g., "Rise Above the Blues," "There's a Way Out," "Service: Get a Handle on It," etc.

2. *Challenge Them to Develop Good Habits.* Give each young woman a calendar and 21 stickers. Have them enter their goal for change at the top of the calendar and concentrate on that goal for 21 days. Place the stickers on the calendar the days they tried the new habit. It takes 21 days to change a habit. If you work consistently for 21 days straight, you have a new habit.

3. *Change Relay:* Have a relay race with a box of clothing in the center. Divide into two teams. Each young woman must run, put on an outfit over her clothing. The outfit includes a skirt and top, a hat, gloves, a belt, and glasses. Then she must model as she walks around a chair four feet away. She must walk back to the box, take off the apparel, and return to her team. All young women could receive a diaper pin pinned on a note that reads: "Prepare for Change."

CHANGE SKIT:
Put on skits (providing bags of clothes). Divide into groups and give them twenty minutes to create skits about change. Then share the skits as you enjoy refreshments.

INTEGRITY — VALUE EXPERIENCE #4: ACTIONS CONSISTENTLY RIGHT

TEMPTATION TRAPS AND ESCAPES BRAINSTORM:
To Make: Print the pattern (shown left) from the *Personal Progress* CD-ROM*. Or, copy or print the pattern from the *Young Women Fun-tastic! Activities – Manual 1* book or CD-ROM (Lesson #28). *Color and cut cards.

Activity: Place a set of the *Temptation Trap* cards in front of young women face down. Ask young women to divide into groups of three or four girls. Have them draw two or more *Temptation Trap* cards. Discuss with your group and write on the card the *Escape Route,* how they can overcome or combat that temptation.

*All images shown in this book can be printed in color or black and white from the

TEMPTATION WEIGHT LIFTING:

Have young women bring some weights (or two cans of soup) and have a weight lifting class. Discuss the weight Satan puts upon us if we accept his temptations. We have the power to push on through any temptation if we "hearken unto the word of God . . . . The fiery darts of the adversary will not overpower us unto blindness or lead us to destruction" (1 Nephi 15:24).

TEMPTATION WHITE BALLOON BOUNCE AND BLACK BALLOON STOMP:

Give each young woman a white and a black balloon to blow up and tie. Tell young women that the white balloon represents purity and the ability to resist temptation and the black balloon represents temptation.

To Play:

1. (White Balloon Bounce): Have young women think of one or two ways they can resist temptation and write it on everyone's balloon with permanent marker. Have young women at the same time bounce their balloons into the air, giving an idea on how to resist temptation, e.g., obey parents, dress modestly, come home from dates early, get enough rest, read the scriptures, pray, attend church, serve others, listen to the Spirit of the Holy Ghost, read *The New Era,* listen to the prophet. Girls can take balloons home.

2. (Black Balloon Stomp): Tell young women that we can "help" each other stomp out temptation by being a good example and sharing the gospel. Give young women a 12-inch string to tie the black balloon to their ankle (with shoes off). At "go," everyone tries to stomp on their neighbor's temptation balloon. When the balloon is popped, she can leave the stomp. The last person with a balloon says, "Help!" and the others can rush back in to stomp out her temptation (balloon).

INTEGRITY — VALUE EXPERIENCE #5: BE AN EXAMPLE

EXAMPLE DECISIONS DRAMA OR DRAW:

To Make: Print the pattern (shown right) from the *Personal Progress CD-ROM**. Or, copy or print the pattern from the *Young Women Fun-tastic! Activities – Manual 1* book or CD-ROM (Lesson #21). *Color and cut out label and wordstrips. Glue label on a bottle and place wordstrips in the bottle.

ACTIVITY: Play this *Example Decisions Drama or Draw* spin-the-bottle game to help young women learn the difference between a positive example of the gospel of Jesus Christ (following in His steps) and a negative example. Take turns drawing a wordstrip from the bottle to act out (DRAMA) or draw (DRAW) the positive and negative example action on the chalkboard.

SHINING EXAMPLE SPOTLIGHT:

You'll need a flashlight for each young woman, 3 x 5 cards, pencils, and art supplies to make thank-you cards. *On the Invitation:* Ask young women to bring a flashlight and a 1-2 minute spotlight, telling of someone who has been a shining example.

Enjoy activities #1-3 as follows.

  Activity #1 Flashlight Spotlight: Start by setting the stage. Turn out the lights and have young women shine their flashlights towards the person giving the spotlight (avoiding her face). Young women can take turns sharing their shining example under the spotlight.

Activity #2 Three Shining Examples: Give each young woman a 3 x 5 card and a pencil to write down three of the shining examples they would like to follow. Before Activity #1, tell young women to listen for three examples they would like to follow.

Activity #3 Thank-You Cards: Using the art supplies, have young women make a homemade thank-you card to send to their shining example.

A RIGHTEOUS EXAMPLE INFLUENCES OTHERS:

Invite young women to talk about people around them who have set righteous examples for them. Discuss what these individuals have done and why it touched them. What did these individuals do that motivated them to feel stronger or more motivated toward good works? Choose three people young women all agree are righteous examples. Then do something as a group to show these people

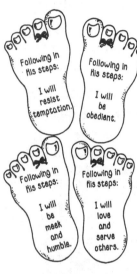

that you appreciate their example (babysit for them, bake and decorate a "thank-you" cake, or wash their car and vacuum it.) The ideas are endless. Write a note and give Hugs candy along with real hugs.

IN HIS FOOTSTEPS MIRROR MOTIVATORS:

Print the patterns (shown left) from the *Personal Progress* CD-ROM*. Or, copy or print the patterns from the *Young Women Fun-tastic! Activities – Manual 1* book or CD-ROM (Lesson #3). *Color and cut out feet.

Activity: Create *Following in His Steps* mirror motivators for each young woman to remind them to walk in the footsteps of Jesus. Post on mirror during the week (one each week). Practice the quality or trait posted on the foot for five days, checking the box and/or painting a toe nail each day with real polish or markers.

WHAT IF? NIGHT:

Use Marion G. Romney's example of solving dilemmas through searching the scriptures and praying. Have a large jar with "What if's" written (e.g., challenging questions but also easy ones, e.g., "What if you get a scholarship to Harvard and BYU?" Or, "What if a friend with questionable standards

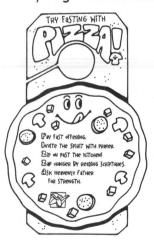

asks you to a party?"). Some can be sensitive questions but still real to today's youth. Be tactful as you search for the Lord's way. Acknowledge that some questions and answers take a lot of searching the scriptures, pondering, and praying.

INTEGRITY — VALUE EXPERIENCE #6: LAW OF THE FAST

TRY FASTING WITH PIZZA! DOORKNOB FASTING REMINDER:

To Make: Print the pattern (shown left) from the *Personal Progress* CD-ROM*. Or, copy or print the pattern from the *Young Women Fun-tastic! Activities – Manual 2* book or CD-ROM (Lesson #23). *Color and cut out.

*All images shown in this book can be printed in color or black and white from the
Young Women Fun-tastic! Personal Progress Motivators CD-ROM.

Activity: Make a *Try Fasting with Pizza!* doorknob hanger for each young woman and read Doctrine and Covenants 88:76. Challenge young women to fast and pray each fast Sunday with a purpose, posting this doorknob reminder on their door to tell the what to do:

"PIZZA: Pay Fast Offering. Invite the Spirit with Prayer. Zip on Past the Kitchen!.
Zap Hunger By Reading Scriptures.
Ask Heavenly Father for Strength."

• *Optional Idea—Fasting Facts:* Gather information and quotes from Church leaders on the proper way to fast, why we fast, and what happens to the body and spirit when we fast. The *Ensign* and *Era* are great sources.

• *Optional Idea—Fast Together with a Purpose:* Select a purpose to fast, either individually or as a group. Young women might choose to fast for a young woman they wish to fellowship and activate, a need in the ward or community, or someone's illness or physical challenge. Make a list of reasons to fast. Discuss Queen Esther, who fasted to save her people (Esther 4-5).

INTEGRITY — VALUE EXPERIENCE #7: PROBLEMS THAT WEAKEN THE FAMILY

See Divine Nature — Value Experience #2: QUALITY WIFE AND MOTHER,
#3: MAKE HOME LIFE BETTER, AND #5: STRIVE TO OBEY PARENTS

DRUG ABUSE (DRUG FREE ME! WORD FIND):
To Make: Print the pattern (shown right) from the *Personal Progress* CD-ROM*. Or, copy or print the pattern from the *Young Women Fun-tastic! Activities - Manual 1* book or CD-ROM (Lesson #39). *Color.
ACTIVITY:
1. Complete the *Drug Free Me!* puzzle to find drug names: marijuana, tobacco, caffeine, LSD, cocaine, crack, alcohol, heroin, barbiturates, amphetamines, diet pills.
2. Write below ways you plan to resist and not give in to taking drugs: peer pressure, escape, immaturity, availability, advertising appeal.

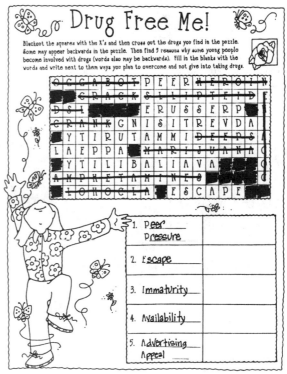

DRUGS QUESTION AND ANSWER SESSION:
Have a qualified police officer, e.g., from the DARE Program, come in and talk to young women about drugs. Have a question and answer brainstorm before the officer comes, with one or two young women presenting these questions. Encourage young women to ask questions there. Bake a plate of yummy but healthful treats for the officer with a note of appreciation signed by the girls. Quick Treat Ideas: Make a poster warning against drugs, using candy bars, e.g., Create "Joy" - Keep Off Drugs (Almond Joy bar). If young men are invited, give them a Big Hunk candy bar and say "Be a Big Hunk and say 'no' to drugs."

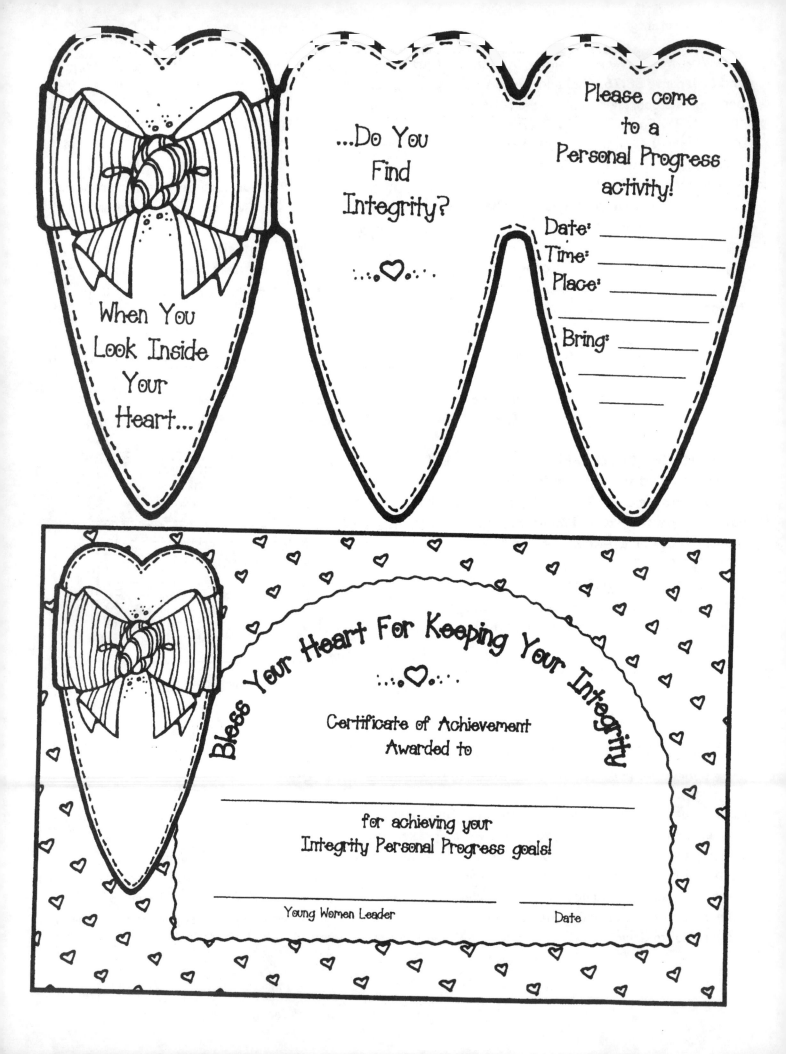

When You Look Inside Your Heart...

...Do You Find Integrity?

...·♡·...

Please come to a Personal Progress activity!

Date: _____
Time: _____
Place: _____
_____
Bring: _____
_____
_____

Bless Your Heart For Keeping Your Integrity

...·♡·...

Certificate of Achievement
Awarded to

_____

for achieving your
Integrity Personal Progress goals!

_____
Young Women Leader

_____
Date

Standards for the Strength of Youth

Integrity – Value Experience #1:

SEARCH AND PONDER:

Moroni 10:30-33

After reading this scripture I thought about what it means to "deny yourselves of all ungodliness" as follows:

_____

_____

SEARCH AND PONDER:

"Standards for the Strength of Youth"
(page 2-4 in Personal Progress booklet)

I reflected on how the Lord's standards differ from the world's standards as follows:

Lord's Standards: The World's Standards:

_____

_____

_____

My Personal Standards for Actions I kept for 1 month:

Dress: _____   Literature: _____

Movies: _____   Television: _____

Internet: _____   Music: _____

Conversation: _____   Morals: _____

My Plan to stay morally clean and worthy to attend the temple is:

_____

_____

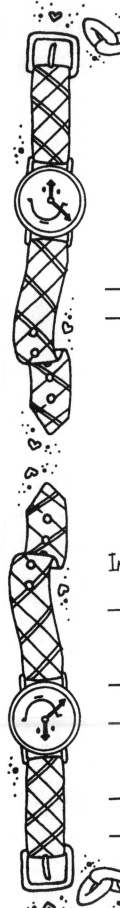

Time for a Change in Personal Behavior

Integrity — Value Experience #2:

I selected the following personal behavior I wish to change:

_____

_____

Ideas: avoiding gossip or inappropriate jokes,
avoid swearing and profanity, be truthful and honest,
being morally clean, avoid being light-minded about sacred subjects,
being dependable, be trustworthy in work and school work
and with other activities with friends

I Prayed Daily for the Holy Ghost to Help Me Live with

Integrity (My Thoughts): _____

_____

My Goal and Attempts to Change this Behavior:

_____

_____

My Feelings about Living with Integrity:

_____

_____

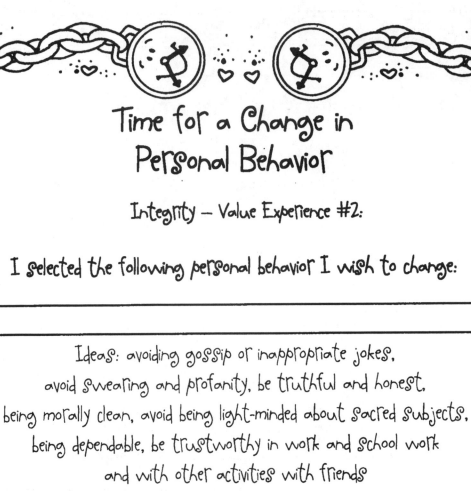

Courage to Show Integrity

Integrity – Value Experience #3:

I Studied the Following Individuals Who Showed Courage.
Here Are Three Ways Each Has Shown Integrity:

Joseph in Egypt (Genesis 39): _____
_____

Esther (book of Esther): _____
_____

Daniel (Daniel 3 and 6): _____
_____

Apostle Paul (Acts 26): _____
_____

Hyrum Smith (D&C 124:15): _____
_____

Joseph Smith (Joseph Smith—History 1:21-25): _____

A Time When I Had Courage to Show Integrity, Especially When it Was Not Popular:

_____
_____
_____
_____

(I shared the above experience in a testimony meeting, lesson,
or with a parent or young women leader.)

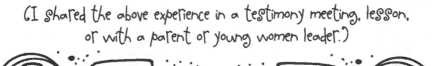

right! Dare to

Make Your Actions Consistently Right

Integrity – Value Experience #4

___ I Looked up the Word Integrity in the Dictionary to Learn the Definition: _____

_____

Words to describe: Honor, honesty, standards, character, reliability, good, right, righteousness

I Interviewed My Mother ___, Grandmother ___, or Another Woman ___ by the Name of _____
About Her Understanding of the Word Integrity as Follows:

_____

_____

The Following Are Ways I Can Make My Actions Consistent with My Knowledge of Right and Wrong:

I can: _____

when tempted to: _____

I can: _____

when tempted to: _____

I can: _____

when tempted to: _____

"Bee" a Better Example

Integrity – Value Experience #5:

SEARCH AND PONDER:

Mosiah 18:9
This Scripture Tells Me How to Stand as a Witness of
God at all times and in all things . . .
That [I] may have eternal life.

I Chose the Following Personal Behavior That I Need
To Improve on So I Can Be a Better Example:

_____

_____

_____

I practiced this behavior for two weeks:

Week #1: M __ T __ W __ T __ F __ S __ S __

Week #2: M __ T __ W __ T __ F __ S __ S __

My Experiences:

_____

_____

_____

_____

_____

Live the Law of the Fast

Integrity — Value Experience #6:

___ I practiced integrity by living the law of the fast on a fast Sunday: _____,

___ I abstained from food and drink for two consecutive meals. Breakfast ___, Lunch ___, or Dinner ___.

I Had a Specific Purpose in Mind as I Fasted: _____

_____

_____

Ideas or Purposes for Fasting: Fast for a Sick Friend,
To Overcome a Bad Habit, Obtain Special Help or
A Blessing for Myself or Someone Else, Give Thanks

___ I Opened and Closed My Fast with Prayer.
Things I Prayed About: _____

_____

_____

_____

_____

_____

_____

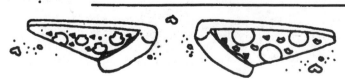

Trends and Problems
that Weaken a Family

Integrity – Value Experience #7:

SEARCH AND PONDER:

the First Presidency message
(on page 1 of the Personal Progress booklet)

From this First Presidency Message I Discovered the Issues,
Trends, and Problems That Weaken the Family as Follows:

_____

_____

_____

_____

I Researched a Church Magazine to Learn Counsel from
Today's Prophet Regarding the Family as Follows:

_____

_____

_____

I Shared the Following (My Plan to Strengthen the
Home and Family) with My Leaders or Parents:

_____

_____

_____

Integrity Value Project Planner

My Project Is:

_____

_____

_____

Steps to Carry Out My Project:

1. _____
2. _____
3. _____
4. _____
5. _____
6. _____
7. _____
8. _____

How I Felt about the Project:

_____

_____

How My Understanding of Integrity Increased with this Project:

_____

_____

_____

Appendix:

Patterns for 1 and 2 follow:

1. Personal Progress Value Quilt

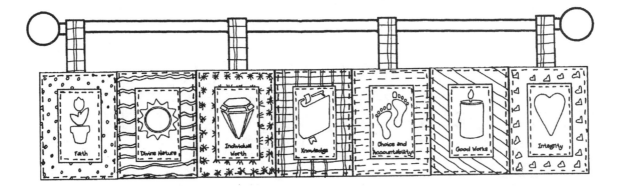

2. Journal cover page and tabs

How to Make the Personal Progress Value Quilt

This Value Quilt can be given to young women, one quilt block at a time as they complete all their Personal Progress goals for that value. For example, when they complete all their Faith goals they can obtain the Faith quilt block (shown right and below) to sew onto their quilt. Make the quilt ahead of time and mount it on the dowels so young women can hang it in their room. This will remind them to achieve all of their Personal Progress goals to obtain all of the quilt blocks.

Faith

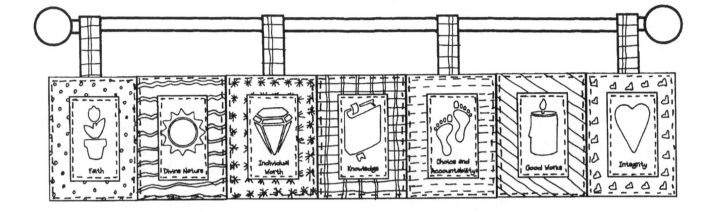

Viewing the quilt left to right you will find the Personal Progress symbols. Symbols are also found on the invitations and certificates in this book and CD-ROM.

Steps to Making the Value Quilt:

1. Cutting Out: Using the patterns provided on the following pages, cut the seven different quilt pieces, back piece, and fabric loops. Cut out and tear the muslin to the size stated on the pattern. Also, cut the piece of quilt batting.

Note: Pre-wash each piece of fabric separately before cutting pieces. This will keep the colors from bleeding if quilt needs to be washed.

SUPPLIES NEEDED:
- Fabric: Different print scraps with a dominant background the color of each of the values. Faith (white), Divine Nature (blue), Individual Worth (red), Knowledge (yellow), Choice and Accountability (orange), Good Works (green), and Integrity (purple)
- Muslin for value stencil pieces
- Fabric for the back (24 ½" x 5 ½")
- Quilt batting the same size as the back piece
- A 24" dowel (of choice) with end attachments
- Needle and thread
- Sewing machine
- Copy of stencils on cardstock paper or plastic stencil sheets
- Acrylic paint
- Textile medium
- Artist's spray adhesive
- Sponge or sponge brush
- Fine laundry marker

2. Make Four Fabric Loops: With wrong sides together, sew a 1/4" seam up the long side. Then turn loop outside right and press flat. Fold loop in half and press flat again. Repeat with other three pieces.

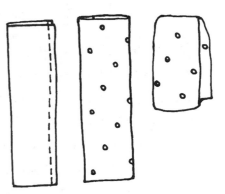

3. Make the Quilt Front: Use the seven value color quilt blocks, start with the white and blue quilt blocks first. Put right sides together, sew a 1/4" seam up the longest side of the blocks. Open the quilt blocks right side up and then place the red quilt block face down on the blue block and sew an identical seam up the right side. Lay open the three quilt blocks and place the green block face down on the red block and sew up the right side again. Continue using the orange, yellow and finally purple blocks until all are connected. Press the entire strip of quilt blocks flat with seams open.

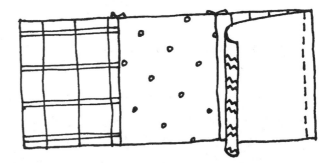

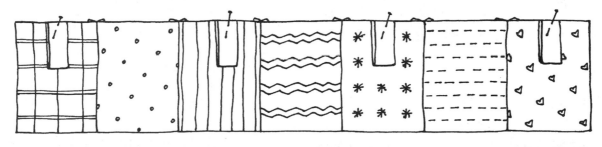

4. Put the Quilt Together (shown above): Lay down the quilt blocks, right side up. Position the four fabric loops, folded end downward, in the center of the first, third, fifth, and seventh blocks as shown and pin in place. Then lay the back piece right side down—directly on top of the quilt blocks and the quilt batting on top of the back piece. Pin in place around all sides. Sew a 1/4" seam around the entire quilt leaving approximately three inches along the bottom edge. Open to turn the quilt right side out. Before turning right side out, carefully trim the batting on the outside of the seam as close to the seam as possible to keep corners and edges from being too bulky. Turn quilt right side out.

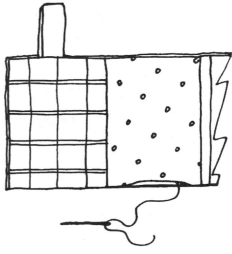

5. Press the quilt edges flat, including the open seam as if it were stitched. With a needle and thread, close the opening with a whip stitch, holding the stitches.

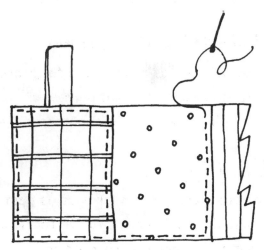

6. Using a quilt stitch (shown right), sew 1/4" in from the edge on each of the blocks as shown. Complete on each of the other six quilt blocks. The quilt is now ready to hang.

7. Glue the wood ends to the dowel and let dry. Once dry, pass the dowel through the four fabric loops to hang.

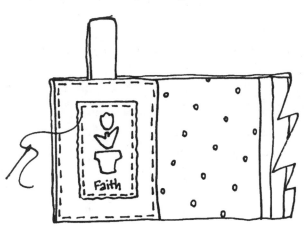

8. When each of the young women have completed the requirements for a particular value, the value stencil piece is awarded. Each of the girls can sew their award to the corresponding value colored quilt block on their quilt. To attach the value stencil piece (shown right), pin in place on the center of the quilt block. Stitch 1/4" in from the edge using the quilt stitch. The stencil piece has a raw edge and does not need to be tucked under. The raw edge is part of the charm of this quilt. The edge can be frayed, or if the stencil piece was torn (instead of cut), it will already appear to be frayed.

How to Create and Use the Stencils:

- Each value stencil has been divided into the different colors that will be stenciled.
- Some values may have only one stencil, e.g., the value Integrity has only one, while Good Works has three.
- The blackened area is the area to be cut out. Using an Exacto knife, carefully cut out along the edge leaving open only the area that is to be painted and covering the other areas.

Creating the Stencils:

You can create the stencils by copying or printing them on cardstock paper. Cut out the areas in black only. You can also use plastic sheets purchased at any craft store that are created especially for stencils. You will need to trace the area to be cut out onto the plastic sheet and then with an Exacto knife, cut out the area to be painted. Plastic sheets allow for easier placement, since they are fairly transparent; but you can also easily position stencils created on the cardstock paper using a light box or holding it up to a window.

To Make the Paint for Stenciling:

Any acrylic paint is appropriate for stenciling. However, since you are creating a washable quilt, you will need to make the paint permanent by adding a textile medium. Follow the directions according to the textile medium you have purchased in regard to the ratios of medium paint.

Stenciling Tips:

• To keep stencil form slipping, it is best to use a light coat of artist's spray adhesive on the back of the stencil. It will adhere to the fabric and can be peeled off once the paint has been applied.
• When the stencil is positioned on the cut material, apply the paint with a sponge or sponge brush. With a small amount of paint on the sponge or brush, dab the area that has been left uncovered by the stencil. For a clean stencil, be careful not to work any paint under the edge of the stencil during application.
• Make sure the area has dried completely before painting another portion of the stencil.

Writing the Value Names:

The value names are on the stencils. You can write the names by placing the stencil on the back of the fabric and using a light box or window to trace the letters with a fine tip laundry marker.

THE PATTERN SHOWN RIGHT IS TO BE COPIED ALONG WITH THE OTHER STENCIL PATTERNS THAT FOLLOW:

Integrity

Faith

Faith

Divine Nature

Divine Nature

Individual
Worth

Individual
Worth

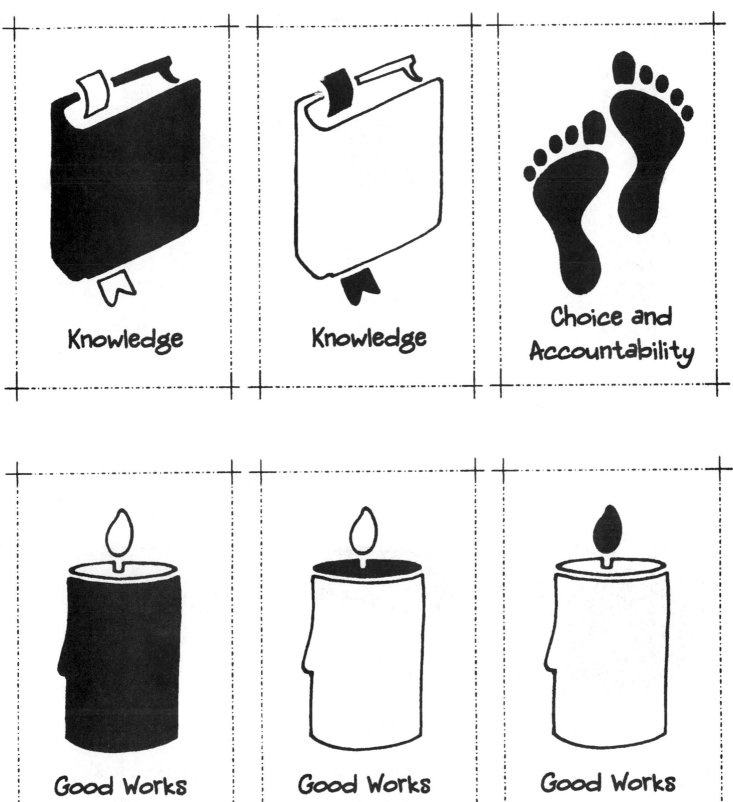

Knowledge

Knowledge

Choice and
Accountability

Good Works

Good Works

Good Works

Pattern for
Value Quilt Piece
$\frac{1}{4}$" seam allowance

Dimensions: 4" X 5 $\frac{1}{2}$"

Cut 7
(One of each
value color)

Pattern for
Value Quilt Piece
$\frac{1}{4}$" seam allowance

Dimensions: 4" X 5 $\frac{1}{2}$"

Cut 7
(One of each
value color)

Pattern for Value
Stencil Piece with
Unfinished Edge

Dimensions:
2 ¼" X 3 ¾"

Cut or tear 7
for each quilt

Pattern for Value
Stencil Piece with
Unfinished Edge

Dimensions:
2 ¼" X 3 ¾"

Cut or tear 7
for each quilt

Pattern for Fabric Loop
¼" seam allowance

Dimensions: 2 ½" X 6"

Cut 4 for each quilt

Pattern for Fabric Loop
¼" seam allowance

Dimensions: 2 ½" X 6"

Cut 4 for each quilt

Young Women Fun-tastic! Activities
Lesson Lifesavers for Manuals 1, 2, and 3

All books are also available on CD-ROM to print images in color or black and white.

Looking for new and exciting ways to teach your Young Women about service, goals, honesty, charity, gospel standards, self-mastery, testimony, and other aspects of the gospel? Look no further than these treasure-trove collections of great ideas. Each activity is listed alphabetically and cross-referenced to a particular lesson in the Young Women Manuals 1, 2, and 3.

Teachers and young women alike will love the fun and unique ideas and activities contained in these books. And teachers will especially enjoy the simple, creative, memorable ways their young women can learn important gospel principles.

With clever handouts as well as games and crafts, *Young Women Fun-tastic! Activities:* Lesson Lifesavers for Manuals 1, 2, and 3 will be a hit with everyone!

Meet the Creators of the Young Women Fun-tastic! series:

Mary Ross, Author

Jennette King, Illustator

They are also the creators of the popular *Primary Partners* series and more: *Gospel Fun Activities* and other family home evening books and CD-ROMs. Mary lives in Sandy, Utah with her husband Paul and daughter Jen, and Jennette lives in Riverton, Utah with her husband, Clayton and two sons, Levi and Carson.